Back from the Dead

Back from the Dead

THE BOOK OF CONGREGATIONAL GROWTH

GERALD W. KEUCHER

Morehouse Publishing
NEW YORK · HARRISBURG · DENVER

Morehouse Publishing, 4775 Linglestown Road, Harrisburg, PA 17112

Morehouse Publishing, 445 Fifth Avenue, New York, NY 10016

Morehouse Publishing is an imprint of Church Publishing Incorporated.
www.churchpublishing.org

Cover design by Laurie Klein Westhafer
Illustrations by Jay Sidebotham
Typeset by Vicki K. Black

Library of Congress Cataloging-in-Publication Data
Keucher, Gerald W.
   Back from the dead: the book of congregational growth / Gerald W. Keucher.
      p.   cm.
   Includes bibliographical references.
   ISBN 978-0-8192-2806-2 (pbk.: alk. paper) — ISBN 978-0-8192-2807-9 (ebook)
   1. Church renewal. I. Title.
BV600.3.K48 2012
254'.5—dc23   2012005934

Printed in the United States of America

TO NATALIE AND MIA

May you live to see your children's children;
may peace be upon Israel. (Psalm 128:6)

and in memory of
MARTHA LEWIS KEUCHER
the best mother any boy could ever have

Contents

Acknowledgments

I am deeply grateful to the people of the Church of the Intercession, New York City, and to the staff, the Reverend Fred Hoyer Johnson, Jr., the Reverend Nora Smith, the Reverend Ivan Griffith, William E. Randolph, Jr., Tommy Cheng, Eduardo de la Fuente Farías, Juliet Lowe-Tannis, and Richard Freeman for their friendship and for the work we did together. I cannot think of Intercession without thanking God for all of them. Together we truly looked into the abyss and, by God's grace and the prayers and devotion of everyone, kept that magnificent place from falling in. Wow.

I am also grateful to the people of St. Mary's, Brooklyn, another back-from-the-brink situation where I now serve. As always, the staff—Elizabeth Greaves, Charlie Monico, and Mark Victor Smith—make it possible for good things to happen. My work at St. Mary's is proving the hypothesis I brought to the work: there is a method to turning around a place at the brink of failure.

Intercession was not the first parish I saw come back from the dead. In 1982, long before I was ordained, my partner, priest, and iconographer John Walsted, became priest-in-charge and then rector of Christ Church, Staten Island, a beautiful complex then in a seriously weakened state. The diocesan office had urged a merger with another struggling parish several miles distant, but the lay leaders of both were unwilling to pursue that option. During John's tenure, we learned by trial and error both what and what not to do. There was no miracle of sudden growth; there was the work of welcoming, incorporating, educating, articulating a vision, reaching out, raising money, forming stewards, doing pastoral care, running a moderate-size capital campaign, asking for planned gifts, building the endowment—all the normal things, but made as effective as our gifts would allow by John's patent goodwill and his overflowing love for the parish. At his retirement service, a parishioner said it had been a magic time, and I realized that, however important *what* we did had been, the attitude and spirit John had brought and fostered was even more vital.

My years at the diocesan office in New York gave me opportunities to observe and think about what was working, what wasn't, and what might be more effective. I came away with two deep convictions, each of which led to a book. First, unless leaders understand their responsibility to the future, they will make decisions that will shortchange and perhaps foreclose that future. Second, unless leaders at the parish and diocesan levels bring true mutual accountability to all their relationships, they will abuse the powers of their offices and weaken the part of the church they should be building up.

A book like this cannot be the product of one mind or one person's experiences. I want to thank those clergy who have helped me directly with this book, either through conversations about their work or by providing examples over the years that I have remembered. A few among the many are the Reverends George Adamik, Hilario Albert, Randy and Patty Alexander, Ken Brannon, Diane Britt, Jerry Brooks, Jim Burns, Joe Campo, David Carlson, Ethan Cole, Roy Cole, Dale Cranston, Peter Cullen, Gawain de Leeuw, Michael Delaney, Terry Elsberry, Judith Ferguson, Doug Fisher, Susan Fortunato, Clarke and Sally French, Frank Geer, Bill Geisler, Richard Gressle, Tobias Haller, Lynn Harrington, Fred Hill, Chuck Howell, Frank Hubbard, Betty Hudson, Allan Jackson, Joan Jackson, Earl Kooperkamp, Larry LeSeure, Kathleen Liles, Elliott Lindsley, Lucia Lloyd, Carl Lunden, Richard Marchand, Tom Margrave, John Merz, Glenworth Miles, Loyda Morales, Andrew Mullins, Tom Newcomb, Tom Nicoll, Martha Overall, Carrie Schofield-Broadbent, Fred Schraplau, Bob Shearer, Michael Sniffen, Buddy Stallings, Herb Stevens, Astrid Storm, Barry Swain, Bill Tully, Don Waring, Richard Witt, Claire Woodley-Aitchison, and the Right Reverends Lawrence C. Provenzano, Scott Barker, Andrew Dietsche, Rodney Michel, and Andrew St. John. Such a bare and informal list is a poor way of expressing the richness of our relationships and our work together. There are so many others as well.

I want to express my deep appreciation to Bishop Provenzano for allowing me the opportunity to serve St. Mary's, Brooklyn, and for demonstrating the kind of visionary strategic thinking that makes a leader agile and supple so that opportunities can be recognized and capitalized on. He also knows how to support and encourage those he supervises.

It is quite impossible to thank the many laypeople with whom I have worked and from whom I have learned so much. One lesson my experiences have taught me is that laypeople are the solution, not the problem, as some clergy prefer to think. I hope this conviction is evident throughout what follows. The fact that the laity resist the latest "innovative model," often offered by clergy or diocesan officials who are not sure what to do, is, in my opinion, generally a good thing. I believe laypeople are the solution, even though I will be mentioning numerous situations in which some lay leaders have acted badly. These actions, I believe, do not arise from personal failings, but rather because these leaders have been part of an unhealthy system. Making the system healthy will allow the people in it to be healthy as well.

I am grateful to Susan Fowler for reading the manuscript and making valuable suggestions.

Finally, it is always a pleasure to acknowledge the supportive team at Church Publishing. When he retired, Frank Tedeschi, a friend of many years, handed me off very smoothly to Nancy Bryan, who has been gracious and helpful. Vicki Black, who edited this manuscript, has ensured that my points are made clearly, and I am very grateful for her contribution to this book.

Staten Island, New York
May 2012

CHAPTER ONE

The Ground Has Shifted

I will lead the blind by a road they do not know,
by paths they have not known I will guide them.
I will turn the darkness before them into light,
the rough places into level ground. These are
the things I will do, and I will not forsake them.
— ISAIAH 42:16

Some years ago I had an experience that changed my life. While I was serving on the administrative staff of the Episcopal Diocese of New York, the Church of the Intercession, a historic parish in northern Manhattan, came close to closing. The physical plant is huge: the footprint of the buildings covers nearly an acre. The endowment had been spent to zero, the buildings had not been maintained for decades, and the once-thriving congregation had dwindled to a faithful few. The insurance on the buildings and on the liability of the parish operation had lapsed for non-payment six years before. Consolidated Edison, the utility that provides electricity and gas in Manhattan, had turned off service to the parish a couple of years previously when the arrearages had reached into the six figures. Although that crisis had been surmounted, the arrival of the

1

monthly utility bill always necessitated an emergency special appeal—in the winter, of course, but almost as acutely during the summer when cash flow dried up. The heating system needed about $250,000 of work or it could not be turned on that fall. There was a lot of conflict in the congregation: one member likened it to a hornets' nest.

It was not at all clear what to do. Intercession had no money at all, and diocesan funds were committed to a program of congregational support that this parish simply would not have fit into. However, it was inconceivable that such a prominent place could be allowed to fail without at least some kind of effort.

A generous parish offered the bishop a grant that would support a priest's compensation for three years. To get a clearer sense of the situation, I looked at the parish budget with the chair of the finance committee. Over $100,000, or more than fifty cents of every dollar of income, was going for heat and light. I could envision no business plan that would make numbers like that work. There was no maintenance staff. A devoted and beloved verger was the sexton, but he was so infirm that opening and closing the buildings was about all he could do.

I reported to the bishop that it made no sense to try to find a priest to take it on. Even if it proved possible to identify someone willing and able to address the situation, a three-year commitment was not long enough to get the parish to the point of being able to pay a full-time priest. And the priest would be able to do almost nothing about rebuilding the membership of the congregation or the parish program because all of his or her time would be spent trying to deal with the latest building crisis or money crunch.

The upshot was that Bishop Sisk asked me to take charge of the parish in addition to my duties as chief financial officer at the diocesan office, with no additional compensation. I served the congregation for almost four years, the first two and a half while still full-time on the diocesan staff and the last sixteen months full-time at the parish.

The experience changed my life, and it changed my head. It was far too much to have agreed to take on. My first thought when the bishop asked me was, "This will kill me," and I was more right than wrong. The stresses and pressures of the two jobs together broke me. This is not an incidental point; we will see that work like this often requires a priest who is willing to be taken advantage of. I survived, however, and the parish was turned around. Here are some things that happened.

§ Individual giving increased by over 75 percent, and total operating income more than doubled. This allowed us to get liability insurance and to fund sufficient maintenance and administrative staff to operate the plant so that additional income could be derived from building use.

§ By finagling and begging and working every system we could, we did the work on the heating system and completed many other capital projects, large and small. With the help of the two best maintenance staffers imaginable, we got control of the buildings and began to catch up with decades of neglect.

§ Members no longer needed to feel apologetic about the way things looked, and outsiders began to want to do things in those great spaces.

§ The parish was able to budget a half-time priest's position, and an excellent priest was found to take over.

§ The loyal members had never given up hope, and now they could see that a future awaited them. There began to be all kinds of ideas about program opportunities, and though there was still a fair amount of squabbling—it's a church, after all—people's heads were in a very different place.

§ Membership and attendance grew—not to any amazing extent, but up every year.

The recovery was fragile when I left and is still fragile. By no means had all the problems been solved; there remain plenty of weaknesses in the operating budget, and the enormous physical plant presents challenges every day. Nevertheless, people had come to understand that there were solutions that could be found. Viable avenues were identified to rebuild an endowment for the capital maintenance of the buildings, which will be necessary for the long-term health of the parish.

Although I presided over this turnaround, I was never under the illusion that it was my handiwork. Too many others made contributions I could not make, including the long-time associate priest and the assistant we hired with the grant about eighteen months into my work. The parish was fortunate to have an extremely gifted organist; I am pretty sure I could not have carried on without the thrilling solace of his music every week.

That was not all. There were possibilities latent in that situation that needed only to be awakened and nurtured, not created. Never before had I felt so deeply my dependence on what God was doing. Never had I seen God's hand so evident as in what was happening in the parish and in the community. For the first time I understood truly what it means to say that things impossible for us are possible for God, and that God's strength is made perfect in our weakness.

It made me want to do it again because it made me see that it could be done.

And it made me want to see if there were things in that experience and in the experiences of colleagues who are in situations of rebirth that might be useful to others in a church where almost every parish seems to be a turnaround situation of some kind. Almost everywhere, it seems, are unsustainable trends that need to be reversed: endowments being depleted and building maintenance deferred, congregations aging and dwindling, budgets that are out of whack because the giving of the membership accounts for too small a percentage, and a rise in interpersonal conflicts stemming from lack of leadership or from previous leadership failures.

WRITING *THE BOOK OF CONGREGATIONAL GROWTH*

The immediate cause of my beginning to write this book was a contribution on a church listserv to a thread on the continuing decline of the mainline churches.

> What I want most is "The Book of Congregational Growth" which like the Book of Common Prayer tells me exactly what to do in my situation to be "missional" for which I was not trained, rather than "caring" for which I was trained. No crying from me because the ground has shifted; I'm waiting for orders. — *The Rev. Canon Richard Brewer, February 2010*

The post was tongue-in-cheek serious, and so is my appropriation of its suggestion for the subtitle of this book. The writer is correct: in years past seminarians of mainline churches were trained to be pastors; they were not trained to be missionaries or redevelopers. The assumption apparently was that the people would be there; clergy just needed to know how to take care of them. Pastoral care, of course, is still of the essence; it's just that there are now other things to do that perhaps did not need to be done before, or did not demand as much time and energy as before.

I have known numerous priests, most now retired or gone, who were ordained around the time the great decline began in the 1960s. In looking at the style of their ministry, I could tell that these men had never been told that they needed to worry about building or keeping a congregation; rather, they should be concerned with making the congregation a force for good and for justice in the community. They devoted themselves to that work. They rehabilitated housing units and devised programs serving thousands of homeless and hungry people. And year by year as attendance diminished, the budget became ever more impossible, and the buildings crumbled, they were surprised and resentful. The rules of engagement were no longer those in force when these clergy had enlisted.

The idea of trying to produce a *Book of Congregational Growth* made me smile, but then it made me think. To attempt a one-size-fits-all book on congregational growth may appear an overreach, but perhaps it's not so unreasonable. After all, the *Book of Common Prayer* intends to be something of a similar nature with regard to the worship of the church. Maybe it is possible to do something like that with respect to how churches get turned around and revitalized.

Of course, first, the Prayer Book does not really tell us "exactly what to do." It provides formulas and structures, but the actual performance of the liturgy will vary from place to place. Architecture, placement of furniture, statues, paintings, decoration, movements, music, number of ministers and acolytes, vestments, crosses, banners, torches, candles, smells, bells—the Prayer Book is largely silent on these matters. The dialogue of the play is there, but detailed stage directions are missing. Yet the liturgy's impact—or lack thereof—depends almost entirely on *how* it is done. And even more than the spaces, ceremonies, and trappings that can be photographed, the way the liturgy touches us depends on the ineffable but unmistakable attitude and spirit conveyed by both the leaders and the assembly.

And second, the Prayer Book doesn't address all liturgical situations. Supplements such as the *Book of Occasional Services* or the old *Manual for Priests* are needed as well. Most clergy have had to come up with liturgical forms for occasions not included in our books. When we do that, we rely on the language and structures the Prayer Book has given us. If, then, the situations discussed here are not entirely like the situation you face, perhaps the observations here can be adapted in the way you have probably adapted prayers and phrases in the Prayer Book to come up with forms for the blessing of animals.

In a sense, the *Book of Congregational Growth* whose contents parallel that of the Prayer Book has largely already been written. Like the "trial use" liturgies that were adapted and compiled into our 1979 Prayer Book, a good bit of *what* to do about congregational growth is already out there. Everyone knows the importance of small groups, prayer, communication, raising the congregation's profile, making the services accessible, incorporating newcomers quickly, emphasizing formation and discipleship, using the internet, and building outreach programs that put people in touch with their desire to be generous.

But congregational growth is not happening—or rather, it is not happening in very many places, and it is not happening enough to overcome the decline that is happening elsewhere. Every year the membership and average Sunday attendance numbers reported in the Episcopal Church and other mainline churches continue their long, slow descent.

I said above that the liturgy consists of three aspects: 1) the dialogue—that is, the words said or sung; 2) the stage directions—that is, the ceremonial used; and 3) the attitude or spirit conveyed by the leaders and the assembly.

This book will not attempt to add significantly to the words of the play, although we will discuss some things I think have been omitted and others that I think have received the wrong emphasis. Nor can this book give you exact stage directions, though I will certainly try to help in that regard. The dynamics of congregations are largely the same, but the circumstances of each one differ from others enough that I cannot write a customary for how to perform the "back from the brink" liturgy in your situation.

In this book I want to concentrate on the third aspect, that is, the spirit that imbues our work. I want to treat what I think the principal reasons are for our continuing inability to turn congregations around despite knowing pretty well what to do. I think the attitude and spirit we convey just are not effective. We are not "doing church" with authenticity or sincerity or conviction—anyway, in many churches today *something* is missing.

"CLOSING THE SALE"

There may have been a time when people went to church for cultural or social rather than religious reasons, but at this point in our cultural history, it is safe to say that just about everyone who walks into one of our parishes is looking for a connection with God. There is now no other reason to enter a church. And God is irresistible. So if every "customer" is ready to buy, and our "product" is irresistible, why do we so frequently fail to close the sale?

Let's think for a minute about those situations we have been in where we have been eager to buy something, but our experience in the store turns us off so completely that we leave without making the purchase that we both intended and wanted to make. What happened? Maybe the selection wasn't there; maybe the price was higher than it should have been. Maybe the store was unkempt, or the lack of signage put us off. Most likely, though, it had to do with the staff. We could not find someone, or the person we found was preoccupied or careless or off-putting or uninformed or defensive or condescending. The attitude conveyed was, "Take it or leave it." We left it.

What about those occasions when we have walked out of a store with something we had not intended to buy? I don't mean that a slick talker snookered us into getting something we didn't need or want. I am talking about when a perspicacious salesperson helped us to realize and find what we were really looking for, and we left grateful for the effort and personalized attention of someone who cared. If that has happened to you, I am confident you have been back to that store.

My perception is that the principal reason our congregations decline and die is that we tend to offer our wares with that "take it or leave it" attitude. For example, a departed friend used to say his fantasy was to have a stone Gothic church with a professional choir and an endowment large enough that the sign out front could say, "Sunday Service at 10:00 a.m. You can come if you want." He was partly joking, of course, but only partly.

Despite how beautiful our buildings and liturgies often are, too many times visitors leave our churches still looking for the connection to God they were hoping to find, and knowing somehow either that they won't find it here or even that they do not want to find it here after the way they were treated. Of course we do not intend to be careless or preoccupied or off-putting or defensive, but something gets in the way, and we fail to offer these visitors a way to make the connection they were looking for. Our performance of the liturgy may have been technically perfect, but it was not effective. That's what I want to try to talk about here.

CAN THIS PARISH BE SAVED?

One thesis of this book is that *places that have declined to the point of extinction can be turned around.* Our decline has been unrelenting, but I contend that it is not inevitable. Congregations that have been overspending the endowment can kick that addictive habit. Seemingly insurmountable building problems can be addressed. Streams of income to fund the operation adequately can be developed. Bare, ruined choirs can once again throng with worshipers. Defeated, demoralized people can catch the vision of a bright future. All these things can happen and are happening, at least in a few places.

I will attempt to be as specific as possible about how these things have come to be because the second thesis of this book is that *these happy developments can be replicated.*

Alas, this is not to say that anyone can replicate them anywhere. Many clergy are not suited to this kind of work. Not every congregation can be saved. And in dioceses where resources are very limited, difficult triage decisions may need to be made. The desirable is not necessarily the vital. These are calls this book cannot make.

My perception is, however, that we may not have needed to throw in the towel as easily as we sometimes have. I met a while ago with the vestry of a historic church in the downtown of a suburban city. The parish had a plant of moderate size in good condition. The congregation was smaller than anybody wanted, but they had some vital ministries. There was considerable anxiety, however, about the fact that they had been running chronic operating deficits for at least fifteen years, and the small "endowment" they had been using to plug the deficits was nearly gone.

Okay, I thought. We need first to find about ten percent more operating income this year and then to explore some ideas for next year's budget. We also need to develop some good practices around the remaining endowment so it can be rebuilt through a planned giving effort. It did not seem that difficult or dire to me.

I learned, however, that the problems seemed insurmountable to them. Their thinking was frozen. They had convinced themselves that the ideas they had already had were everything that could possibly be thought. I have encountered that before. Often, though, people are able to seize on suggestions of new ideas and get started on the road to a better future. So I was surprised when, after we discussed some possibilities, people began to say that they should not be trying to address the budget problem, but rather that they needed to look at "innovative ministry models" involving part-time clergy, yoked situations, and mergers. I think they had been so anxious for so long that all they could imagine was trying to get to a situation where the pressure would be reduced. That seemed to be their motivation for lowering their sights.

The vision of a future, therefore, is very much in the eye of the beholder. The conversation put me in mind of the title of the Luigi Pirandello play, *Così è (se vi pare), (That's the Way It Is [If You Think So]).* There may be situations that I may see teeming with possibilities, but if those involved are too anxious or demoralized to see them even when they are pointed out, the possibilities do not exist. I am pleased to say, however, that following our meeting, that vestry regained its confidence, closed the current year deficit, and has plans for how to address next year's budget.

This leads to a third thesis: *adjusting to decline begets more decline.* So pervasive has been the shrinkage that "managing decline" used to be a skill clergy could put on their computerized profile. However, if we acquiesce to the idea that a congregation cannot grow and cannot generate adequate financial resources and set our sights accordingly, we will not maintain the level we have; rather we will continue to decline. Managing decline is not leadership toward a thriving future.

HOW CAN WE TALK ABOUT THESE MATTERS?

These are difficult things to say in a church where many people have spent decades in parishes in decline. If you are in such a situation as you read this book, you may feel I am blaming you. People involved in a declining parish in a declining church have complicated emotions—sadness, anxiety, nostalgia, denial, anger, guilt, and so many others. If you have been a leader in such a situation, you will likely be coming to another church growth book with some defensiveness as well. And since my thesis is that the decline is largely a result of leadership failures, such defensiveness may seem appropriate.

There is, however, a great difference between assessing responsibility and placing blame. My goal here is to try to find the language that allows us, without getting stuck in blame, recriminations, or defensiveness, to look at difficult questions about our stewardship of the institution and to make changes in what we do—and more importantly how we do it—that will make us more effective.

In order to do this I will say things that challenge the conventional wisdom we have created over the last fifty years. These challenges may be difficult to hear because the conventional wisdom aims at making us feel better about the decline by saying such things as "numbers aren't important," and that economic expedients like yoking two failing parishes are really "innovative ministry models." I believe our conventional wisdom is not serving us well. We need to be able to look at our situation more clearly, although such clarity will show us some discomfiting aspects that are made soothingly indistinct by the rose-colored glasses we have preferred to wear.

WHY IT ISN'T WORKING

I have suggested elsewhere that the mainline churches have failed to respond effectively to the challenges posed by the widespread disappearance of social and cultural pressures that used to promote church attendance.[1] The last gasp of Christendom in most of the United States was the post-World War II return to religion, when, to paraphrase the theme of the popular movie *Field of Dreams,* "we built them, and they came." The silent generation and the baby boomers grew up in this environment and still consider it normative that people should just show up at church, but, as the listserv post I quoted above says, "the ground has shifted." The old maps will not work any longer.

This has been a trend beyond our control, but there are effective adaptations available, and we have not taken the trouble to adapt. Successful adaptations require something other than superficial responses like contemporary music or non-traditional vestments or words projected on a screen. We need rather to change our understanding of ourselves as leaders. We have to think deeply and thoroughly about what it might mean to be an authoritative leader in an institution that now has no social authority. We need to find the authentic authority people saw in Jesus and the early witnesses; we cannot continue to rely on the kind of authority position that the religious institutions of Jesus' day bestowed on the scribes. This rethinking is not comfortable, and our new situation demands more from us than some may be willing or able to give. That is why many clergy are not suited to turnaround ministry.

I have also suggested that we have often mismanaged the patrimony bequeathed to us by our forbears.[2] We have sold property and used the proceeds for operating expenses; we have let our buildings decay; we have depleted endowments and relied too much on other people's money to pay for what we want. It is not easy or comfortable to keep in mind that our principal job as leaders is to hand on to our successors a parish stronger than it was when we began to lead it. In a situation of general decline to say that we are responsible for the success of our successors may seem outrageous.

We have also tended to let ourselves off the hook. The years of pervasive decline have created a deep and reflexive touchiness about numbers or any objective measure of church life. In nearly all discussions of church growth in the Episcopal Church, if someone says numerical growth is possible, desirable, or a mark of a thriving church, others will snap back immediately that *they* will not stoop to play such a crass numbers game; rather, *their* concern for mission, say, or spiritual depth, or whatever, is nobler than that.

And we have set our sights too low. Even congregations that are not in crisis have often been content with inadequate funding that does not inspire the members and keeps the parish from being as effective a witness to the faith as it could be. We need to remember that the only long-term solution to any budget problem is not to cut back on the expense side, but to increase existing sources of revenue and to identify and develop new ones. (And I *do not* mean filling the gap by overspending what's left of the endowment!)

A METHOD,
NOT A CHECKLIST OR A TOOL

I cannot provide a checklist of things that, if done, will guarantee a turnaround. The most I can offer is a method. And this method is less like a procedure, that is, a series of steps, than a way of approaching different situations. Like the family of techniques based on the Stanislavski Method of acting, in which actors draw upon their own experiences, memories, and emotions in their portrayal of a certain character on stage, the method I will propose is something that has to be worked out from within. It is not a utensil that anyone can pick up and use without interior preparation. This method is a way of thinking, a way of relating, and a way of being that keeps first things first and that helps keep our work clear of the baggage that impedes our effectiveness.

I will push the analogy a bit farther. Actors no doubt love applause, but good actors know that the most satisfying praise comes as a by-product of doing a good job. Fundamental to the method I will outline is the idea that gratification has to come from the work of rebuilding the congregation and the institution, not from your rank, the deference shown by others, or the affection people offer you. A leader who goes directly for those pay-offs is like a ham actor who mugs for cheap laughs.

For actors, "working the method out from within" means perhaps ridding oneself of the classical techniques of declamation and facial expressions and gestures that get in the way of an authentic personification of the character. For leaders who want to turn a parish around, it means a similar stripping off of expectations, letting go of our assumptions about how things are "supposed" to be, moving beyond conventional wisdom, and releasing every other external consideration that can keep us from connecting effectively and authentically with the situation at hand.

For example, in one parish that is in the process of being built back up, the staff works hard to produce income from the buildings—tenants, film shoots, parties, events, and so on. More than half of the operating budget needs to come from these sources to operate and maintain a very substantial plant while congregational life revives. A newly-arrived priest, while understanding the necessity of these measures, resents the work and the risk involved. "We shouldn't have to be doing these things," he complains. "People should be giving to support the church." There's a significant difference between having a vision of a thriving self-sustaining congregation, and thinking that there is a certain way things are supposed to work. The former allows us to follow whatever paths might lead to our destination, even if some of the by-ways take us through places where we do not wish to stay. Thinking there is a certain way things are supposed to be causes us to resent the present reality and blinds us to the possibilities for growth that might be latent in our situation but that do not conform to our pre-existing ideas. Ridding ourselves of this way of thinking is one necessary part of following the method we will be discussing.

This method is more about innovative thinking than about replicating techniques. It is about analyzing creatively and strategically the possibilities latent in the actual situation, not about imposing some predefined program that reflects your theological preferences or that seemed to work somewhere else.

In the discussion above I have used the idea of authenticity to describe an actor's impersonation of a character and a church leader's connection with the turnaround situation. I want to offer a word of clarification, because *authenticity* is a word I will use regularly and it can mean different things to different people. When I speak of authenticity in an ordained minister or church leader, I do not mean that we come up with a self-created theological stance or an inner personal style that we then show to the world in an effort to be "authentic." I do not mean putting forward some idiosyncratic way of doing the liturgy or organizing parish life, like a priest I know who lights the rose candle in the Advent wreath on the Fourth Sunday of Advent rather than the Third, simply because it comports better, he says, with his understanding of how Advent leads to Christmas. On entering the parish house of the congregation that priest served, I got a clear sense of his self-presentation before I met him. Everywhere on the bulletin boards and on the doors of the rooms he had posted notes with instructions and reminders, all signed "Father Jim." He is sincere, energetic and committed to his task. His approach, however, is not one I can endorse.

What I mean by authenticity is authenticity in relationship.[3] The authenticity we seek is not the projection of a theological consistency we have created within ourselves. Rather, I mean that others perceive us as authentic when our walk matches our talk. St. Paul puts it this way: "For we do not proclaim ourselves; we proclaim Jesus Christ as Lord and ourselves as slaves for Jesus' sake" (2 Corinthians 4:5). The priest who lights the rose candle on the Fourth Sunday of Advent is proclaiming himself. The authentic witness will live a life that proclaims the acceptance and openness of Jesus. The better we are at living that life, the more we get rid of the baggage that obscures such a transparent identification with Christ.

An "authentic" portrayal of characters on screen or on stage means that the performers have entered so deeply into their roles that the viewers say they have experienced the characters, not the actors playing the roles. After having gone to see *Hairspray* because it starred John Travolta, a friend complained that Travolta had not appeared in the film. That should be, I think, the highest praise for an actor.

I think church leaders should aim for something similar. St. Paul exhorts us to "put on Christ," in much the same way Method actors put on their character. In the church we frequently say we are looking for the Christ in each person. When we are at our best, we are almost transparent. My contention is that the method I have seen used to bring a parish back from the brink will be the more effective the more we have let go of our "church voice" and any other idiosyncratic idea, mannerism, or personality trait that distracts people from Jesus by calling attention to ourselves.

HOW WE WILL PROCEED

Our structures and the ways in which we inhabit them are largely the product of the centuries during which the church was legally, or at least socially,
established. This is no longer the case in our postmodern society, where
the church finds itself increasingly on the cultural margins. The thesis of
chapter 2 is that, while our structures do not necessarily need to be
changed, the way we live in them must undergo drastic transformation if
we are to be effective in a post-Christendom world.

Chapter 3 is an analysis of our conventional wisdom, that is, the way
we talk about ourselves and about what it is reasonable to expect. Many of
the ways we understand ourselves and our situation need to change if our
congregations are to be brought back. If we do not change ourselves and
our approach, we will not be able to lead a turnaround, and the decline
will continue. Chapters 2 and 3 thus provide an introduction to the mental
transformation that is an integral part of the nuts-and-bolts work needed
to reverse the decline in any congregation.

A primary thesis of this book is that the "how" of church turnaround
ministry truly matters: as my mother always said, it's not *what* you do; it's
how you do it. Chapter 4 will look at some of the things we need to have
with us in our toolkit. These "tools" are attitudes, approaches, and styles
that give us the "how" necessary to do effectively the "what" we need to do.

Chapter 5 is about how to organize our thoughts and our work once
we begin in a turnaround situation. And finally, because budgets, buildings,
and interpersonal relationships will be such big parts of what we do in
these churches, each gets its own chapter in chapters 6, 7, and 8.

FILLING IN THE BLANKS

Let's imagine a committed Christian who has never seen a building re-
motely like any Episcopal church, and who has never experienced any kind
of liturgical service of worship. A *Book of Common Prayer* finds its way into
that person's hands. She responds positively—as we want to believe anyone
would respond—to the cadences and images of the liturgies and prayers
we love. And she and her community decide that henceforth they will worship only according to that book.

What would those services look like? If we attended one, we would
know the words, but the service itself would make us giggle or fume—or
probably both—because nothing would look like anything we had seen
before. That community would lack the knowledge of the myriad usages

and customs the Prayer Book assumes we bring to it, and just following the rubrics without that knowledge might lead to confusion.

For example, an uninformed reading of the rubrics might lead to the offerings' being placed on an object called the Altar, as directed on page 361, but the Celebrant might face another piece of furniture called the Holy Table as directed after the *Sursum corda.* An incomplete reading of the rubrics at the Daily Office might lead to something I actually experienced more than once. The rubric says, "One or two Lessons, as appointed, are read" (p. 84). Two long-departed priests had apparently never looked at the subsequent rubric that directs that a canticle be said after each reading (p. 84), so when they officiated, the lessons were read together. Then we stood up and recited the two canticles.

We are in something of a similar situation as we try to navigate the new terrain that has appeared after the ground has shifted beneath us. We still bear the imprint of the assumptions and follow the practices of a former age. We might be able to change those assumptions we become aware of as no longer viable descriptions of this new landscape, but the practices we follow unthinkingly, simply as "the way things are," will trip us up as we try to walk over this new surface.

We are living in a new age. None of us can bring to this *Book of Congregational Growth* the kind of unwritten knowledge that allows us to enact the Prayer Book services. We will grope around for a while. We may run after fads and poorly thought-out expedients. We may be distracted by the attractive lore of other traditions, but for the long term we must find our path deep within our own tradition. Anglicans will simply not be able to ape the evangelicals, for example, who depend so heavily on the person of the leader. For centuries Anglican clergy have been shaped by the knowledge that ordered liturgical traditions are most effective when "the officiant's personality is strictly subordinated to the rite he performs."[4] So how can we be "entrepreneurial" in a stratified and reactive institution that really wants and expects conformity?

It will take us some time to learn the attitudes and approaches we will need to pass on to future leaders. In twenty years, I hope, someone will write a book that contains what will have become the common store of proven practices and attitudes that have rebuilt the Episcopal Church and other mainline churches in the first third of the twenty-first century.

May God grant that it be so.

CHAPTER TWO

New Ways of Living in Our Structures

> *The hand of the LORD came upon me, and he brought me out by the spirit of the LORD and set me down in the middle of a valley; it was full of bones. He led me all around them; there were very many lying in the valley, and they were very dry. He said to me, "Mortal, can these bones live?" I answered, "O Lord GOD, you know."*
>
> — EZEKIEL 37:1–3

If, as I believe is true, we are in a real missionary situation now, then the ways we have behaved since Christianity became the official religion of the late Roman Empire will almost certainly contain many characteristics that will prove unhelpful to our current task. My purpose here is to identify those aspects of our system and ethos I think are in the most need of examination. I do not mean that we need to change our structures, but we need to change the way we inhabit them. The old bones need new flesh and new breath. We cannot continue to operate in our structures as if Christendom still existed.

I use the term *Christendom* in a fairly weak sense. The relationship between church, state, and society has changed in complex ways in the last five hundred years. However, it can certainly be said that until very recently the social order in the West was invested in certain expressions of spirituality. When I say that Christendom no longer exists, I mean, as Charles Taylor puts it, "The spiritual as such is no longer intrinsically related to society."[5] When society operates in a separate realm that in no way depends on the church, then Christendom is well and truly dead.

Here's a small example of what Christendom meant in practical terms. In the early twentieth century through the post–World War II years, Monday newspapers regularly printed news stories—sometimes on the front page—describing the services and sermons of the day before. One would be hard-pressed to imagine finding such a news story about worship services or theological commentary on current events highlighted in today's papers. The only religious news that is now fit to print must involve sex, money scandals, or political controversies.

The disappearance of our voice from the Monday papers is not a sign that there are fewer Christians, just that our voices are not heard as often in the secular press. And not every preacher's words made the news in those former days. The cathedrals and fashionable parishes to which prominent people belonged hogged the headlines. The old WASP ascendancy is dead too; people no longer gather to watch the social elite arrive for their parties.

Evangelicals, storefront pastors, and Roman Catholics no longer accept the notion that cardinal Episcopal rectors and high-steeple Presbyterian ministers are the only ones whose voices should be heard in the news.

If the Christendom initiated by Constantine's edict is a thing of the past, however, we have not returned, as some maintain, to a pre-Constantinian Christianity. Our post-Constantinian situation is more complex, because we must deal with the legacy left by the centuries of Christendom. That legacy includes church buildings of architectural renown that can no longer be maintained, as well as the fallout from strife among Christians and efforts by Christian leaders to control others. People today may not know Jesus, but they do know about Galileo and the Inquisition, the troubles of Northern Ireland, and the Crusades. They know the media outlets and commentators who equate the Christian faith with a right-wing political agenda. We are trying to write fresh insights on a board already covered with an often unhelpful history that cannot be erased or ignored.

THE LEGACY OF ESTABLISHMENT

There is a big difference between an organization unconnected to—and at times oppressed by—the government and one that sees itself as a department of the state, an independent power equal to or above the state, or a necessary part of the culture. Participation in the first is strictly voluntary, but the leaders of the second rely on penal, social, or cultural pressure to gain and keep adherents. The first will be organized to invite new members and to grow; the second will be structured primarily so as to maintain the institution and its place in the power structure of the society, and secondarily so as to control its members.

Since I am devoted to the structures of the Episcopal Church, I hope it will be possible to adapt the ways we live in those structures to our new situation. However, I believe we must recognize first how difficult that adaptation will be, since we will need not only to resist our genetic organizational code, but even to modify it for successful adaptation to occur.

We can say a great deal about the development and elaboration of doctrine from the mid-first century until the beginning of the fourth century, but we know very little about the actual lives and activities of Christian communities. This is not surprising, since Christians were famous for being secretive about such things, and probably intentionally operated under the radar when persecution was always a possibility. Except for some fragments and hints, the *Book of Early Church Life* is missing the dialogue, the stage directions, and the attitude and spirit the churches conveyed that outsiders found so attractive.

Things changed in the fourth century immediately after the Emperor Constantine's embrace of Christianity. The newly privileged church took over the language and forms of the imperial government, in everything from liturgical clothing to buildings for worship. Territories were divided into dioceses and parishes, for example, which were terms of the civil administration. The basilica—still the basic architectural form we have in mind when we think of a "church"—was adapted from the secular governmental buildings then being built.

The church's wagon was quickly and firmly hitched to the horsepower of the government. Within just a few years of the Battle of the Milvian Bridge, Constantine was using imperial force to persecute Christians who dissented from the majority opinion.[6] From then on, through political machinations, mass baptisms, interdicts, inquisitions, persecutions, and executions, our ancestors in the faith generally lost the ability to imagine how the church could exist without the power of the state to coerce obedience.

At the same time, another characteristic of a church of the establishment manifested itself: the wealthy and highborn began to arrogate to themselves the power of the episcopate, "taking with them the mitres which were part of the uniform of the Imperial Court in Byzantium."[7] For example, St. Ambrose of Milan, son of a governor-general, was the imperial governor of the province of Italy before being acclaimed bishop. Had he not been given the episcopate, he might well have become emperor. For centuries afterward, lingering even to the present day, members of leading families felt as entitled to high positions in the church as to those in government and society. At the 2003 General Convention that consented to the election of the first openly gay bishop in the Episcopal Church, a priest whose conservative family had provided generations of clergy and seminary professors to the church was assigned to the same discussion table as I. He saw the vote primarily as an act of *lèse majesté*. If his family did not want it to happen, the rest of us should have refrained out of deference to their generations of leadership.

The Reformation split Christendom in Western Europe, but the reformed churches, from which the mainline churches in the United States mostly descend, were established churches in their countries and continued to depend on their governments to enforce their versions of Christian faith and practice. Even after official persecutions ceased being mounted against non-Anglicans, the indignities of being a Roman Catholic or dissenter in England lingered for centuries.

The purpose of this brief rehearsal of history is meant only to remind us how deeply the established churches and their progeny have been conditioned by the norms and expectations of a close attachment to the social order and a dependence on the power of the state and of the culture. We are still far too enthralled with at least three aspects of the establishment mentality: the titles and adornments of hierarchy, a preoccupation with the institution itself, and the seductive power of coercion.

OBSESSION WITH HIERARCHY

In all church denominations newly ordained clergy embark on an assumed career path that may start out modestly as an assistant or associate minister, but should end as the leader of a big parish or in a position at a "higher" level of the denomination. Even those who do not accept that path as inevitable must find a way to live in a system where most people do, so it is considered noteworthy, and perhaps pitiable, if someone steps off that track. For example, nearly fifty years ago when my uncle, an American Baptist minister, resigned as the executive minister of a state convention to return to being the pastor of a congregation, many friends and colleagues were surprised, although the congregation was a prominent one. Clergy who spend their ministries in small places are justifiably self-conscious because they often are the objects of pity or condescension.

Here is a good example of the problem. When a friend recently left a small city parish to take on a rural congregation that needed redevelopment, a bishop said to him, "Well, you've certainly taken yourself off the ambition track." "I didn't know that's what I was on," he replied. My friend's decision was right in every way. Here was work he loved and at which he is particularly effective, in a place that wanted his gifts. The bishop's comment stung. The insensitivity of the bishop's remark is not what is most telling; rather, it is the bishop's assumption that the desire for advancement—more central place, better title, higher pension base, purple piping or a miter—is the normal and expected driver of our decisions, not the desire to do what we love passionately in the contexts that best suit our vocations.

We have developed religious language to obscure the problem of ambition. We speak of gifts, discernment, desire for wider service and such. The line between an aspiration to use one's gifts and the pursuit of an office for its own sake is difficult to draw, but it is there. No doubt in many cases the desire to serve is genuine. In many other cases, however, there is also that urge to be recognized, to retire with the highest possible pension, to get one over on others, and especially to be in a position where you do not have to hold yourself accountable to others. The proof of the pudding will be in the eating, but in the case of bishops and rectors, once you've ordered that particular dish and found it unpalatable, it cannot be returned easily—if at all.

We all know there are bishops and rectors who have carefully "worked" the career ladder to arrive where they wanted to be. This has led some to observe, only partly facetiously, that evincing a desire to be a bishop is *prima facie* evidence of unsuitability for the office.

Ambition will remain a problem, however, because greatness is seldom thrust upon us. As we have seen, even Ambrose was not summoned from nothing. In any institution the palm is awarded to those who come forward to grasp it or to those whose connections can secure it. Many will be worthy, but those who choose from among the contestants need to be more careful than they have been, in many cases. For the sake of a church in urgent need of rebuilding, it is more necessary than ever both to weed out those with "purple fever" who seek high office but lack the vision and leadership skills we need today, and to prevent them from rising to positions beyond their level of competence.

The operation of this Peter Principle, which posits that all employees within a hierarchy tend to be promoted until they reach their level of incompetence, will cause a successful corporation to stagnate and will prevent a declining church from being rebuilt. The church suffers from a chronic lack of mutual accountability throughout our system because our conventional wisdom tells us that objective ways to measure performance are suspect. So it is easy for ambitious clergy to use glib words to get to the next rung on their career ladder, while papering over dangerous weaknesses in their past performance. The current procedures we use to elect bishops and call clergy to parish and institutional positions encourage the ambitious to put themselves forward and "sell" their suitability for a position in ways that would have been thought unseemly in the past. And given what has happened within the leadership ranks of more than a few dioceses in recent years, it would be difficult to maintain that the current system is working that well.

The church is and must continue to be an institution. Organized religion is the only kind there is. And institutions are inherently hierarchical. And yet, while I believe these statements are true, I also believe that we know that God did not take on human flesh in order to create a hierarchical institution of social control. I think we sense with Charles Taylor in his discussion of the maverick Roman Catholic priest, Ivan Illich, that "something is lost when we take the way of living together that the Gospel points us to and make of it a code of rules enforced by organizations erected for this purpose." We intuit that Jesus did not come to reveal universal rules about how we ought to live, but rather "a new way of being. This involves on one hand a new motivation, and on the other, a new kind of community." The Gospels and the Acts of the Apostles depict, not a centralized, reactive institution, but what Taylor calls a "network of agape" that subverts all normal kinship groups and social boundaries. "The corruption of this new network comes when it falls back into something more 'normal' in worldly terms."[8]

No doubt it would have been impossible to maintain a non-hierarchical agape network around the world for millennia. We need our hierarchies, perhaps for the same reason Jesus' interlocutors needed Moses to have provided for the possibility of divorce in the law: our hearts are very hard indeed. And such institutions may have been able to survive and thrive when Christianity had the support of the culture, if not the state.

However, the church is no longer an institution that can take survival and public support for granted, as the churches of Christendom could. The ecclesiastical games that delight Trollope's readers are still being played, but now their effects are less amusing. Lust for position, thirst for power, and avoidance of accountability now hurt the church at all levels in ways that are increasingly difficult to repair. These are aspects of church culture and practice we must stalwartly resist. Now especially we need to have effective and conscientious leaders who are inspired and supported in the work they love in places to which they are suited. A good bit needs to change in us before that becomes the typical way we operate in our structures.

PREOCCUPATION WITH THE INSTITUTION

There is no doubt that the mainline churches are preoccupied with the institution in ways that hinder growth and redevelopment, and here I am not talking about buildings or finances. A church that is part of the social and cultural establishment is more likely to urge faithful participation in the rites of the church and faithful obedience to its structures than to stress personal appropriation of the effects of the members' experiences of God. For this reason critics of the Episcopal Church said in the early nineteenth century that we were "all Church and no Christ."[9]

Moreover, we can find ourselves using the church as a proxy for our own experience and practice. For example, when I suggested to a rector that she commend proportional giving, she replied, "Oh, we already do that. Ten percent of our budget goes to outreach"—as if that were sufficient. Or, many parishes have separate 501(c)(3) corporations that provide needed services through government contracts. The priest will talk about the parish's commitment to these programs, but usually very few parishioners are involved in the ministry. Often the parish's only involvement is to receive the rent checks the outreach corporation pays for use of the church's space. The work of the institution is a necessary outgrowth of, but not a substitute for, the involvement of individual members in being generous stewards and advocates of justice. That's where transformation occurs.

If the mainline churches are not skilled at evangelism, there is a very good historical reason. The American offspring of the established churches of Europe did not need to attract members when government sanctions, ecclesiastical threats, or social expectations could compel, or at least entice, people into the doors. And the evangelical fervor of the Methodists and Baptists has cooled after nearly two centuries of being part of the cultural establishment of this country. Episcopal clergy in the New York of the early 1800s were said to be

> more orderly than zealous—more orthodox than evangelical—more distinguished for attachment to the ritual of the Church than for a fervent and edifying mode of performing it—more intent upon guarding their folds against the inroads of enthusiasm than upon the conversion of sinners.[10]

This may be another way of expressing what Canon Brewer meant by saying he was trained to be pastoral, not missional. Order, orthodoxy, conformity, and predictability are precisely what an institution of the establishment seeks. Clergy were trained to be good soldiers, loyal subjects, organization men—in short, solid sextons of the status quo.

It has become commonplace to say that an entrepreneurial spirit is necessary for clergy who are starting or re-starting congregations. I believe this is true, but we have not thought through the implications of introducing that spirit into a system that is still all about maintenance and conformity. Almost by definition entrepreneurs are more comfortable outside bureaucratic institutions; inside those institutions, they do not make good soldiers who carry out orders and refer the difficult and interesting decisions to higher pay grades.

We use our structures in ways that are highly reactive and lack mutual accountability. In one diocese it was a standing joke that you did not want your name to be mentioned in a diocesan staff meeting, since only acute problem situations were ever discussed in that setting. There was no capacity to think strategically, no desire to examine things that were working to see if they could be replicated, no consideration of how to address seriously declining situations if they were not in a full-blown crisis. There was no thought of supporting or even thanking those who were working effectively. If the situation was not actually a conflagration, there was no need to deal with it. The pope is in perfect health until he dies.

It is possible to be both an entrepreneur and a team player, but leading such clergy effectively will require something quite different from the reactive, unaccountable style which is the default diocesan position. The bishop and staff need to be entrepreneurial in the same healthy way—strategic thinkers who cultivate relationships of mutual accountability and who are not wedded to their own ideas. They need to take responsibility for their actions and to be able to apologize for mistakes and missteps without defensiveness or blaming the victim. They need to be open to the opportunities that serendipitously present themselves, able to choose the right people and then to inspire and support them in their work. Without inspiration team players will lose the entrepreneurial spirit; without support entrepreneurs will become lone rangers. I emphasize that if either of these occur, it is a sign of failure on the part of the diocesan leadership, not the priest—who will no doubt be blamed.

THE SEDUCTIVE POWER
OF COERCION

A church with a Christendom mentality will inevitably be more about control than about conversion. As a part of the apparatus of government and society, its concern will be to train up loyal subjects who accept their immutable place in the social order. Even with that civil support gone, a Christendom church—progressive or traditionalist—will still frame its views in terms of obligation. "Conservatives" can speak in the language of obligation about what we must believe or how we must act. "Liberals" can try to enforce a kind of political correctness: for example, only inclusive language is acceptable; other idioms must be excluded. Most Christian leaders are in fact encouraged in their training to try to remake and reform the people and parishes they serve. We will discuss another way to approach that in the final chapter.

With the power of government behind it, an establishment church will enforce its faith and order in whatever ways may seem expedient. Elizabeth I's desire not to "make windows into men's souls" was certainly more theologically modest—and politically astute—than the inquisitor's rack, but torture and execution for religious deviancy were hardly rare in Tudor England, and Elizabeth was just as likely to turn to these means of control as her father had been when she deemed it necessary.

The more a church understands itself as part of the establishment, the more it will rely on threats of punishment and promises of rewards to enforce its rules. The church begins to see itself as the treasure rather than the earthen vessel in which the treasure resides. No longer a minister of the grace of God, the church becomes the definer of grace, setting the limits, saying who is acceptable and who is not. Establishment churches will want their preferences legislated so that all must bend to their will.

Although the mainline churches have generally ceased threatening hell and promising heaven, we are by no means done with the more subtle use of coercion. Our language is still far more often the language of obligation than the language of invitation.

Some years ago in a small parish after a service during which I had preached on proportional giving, an elderly woman said, "That was the first sermon I ever heard about money that didn't make me mad." I expressed my gratitude, and we chatted. The significance of her words struck me only as I was driving home. Here was a woman who had been in church every Sunday for eighty years or more. She had heard hundreds of sermons about money from many different priests, *and they had all made her mad!*

It is not too difficult to realize what makes people angry when we talk about money. Usually we communicate a sense of urgency, if not panic, because there's never enough money. That makes people anxious, and many find it annoying to be made anxious year after year. We also almost always communicate a sense of obligation: you should, you have to, you need to, you ought to contribute more than you are giving. If those are not the words we use, perhaps we switch to the passive-aggressive mode: "God is calling us to give more." While it would no doubt make our life easier if people gave more, perhaps God is not calling the people to respond to our guilt-inducing, self-serving language.

Our concerns with the hierarchy and the position of the institution are probably matters that distract the clergy and lay leaders from their task more than people in the pews, but our use of the language of obligation and other forms of coercion is where we make our members understand that we are acting as if Christendom still existed. You must attend church for six months before your baby can be baptized; you have to do the Alpha program before you can be married here; we won't nominate anyone for the vestry who has not completed a Cursillo weekend. You should increase your pledge by $20 a week in order to help cover the budget deficit.

It's time to reach back into the centuries when Christianity was an often despised minority. The words of a hymn, based on a text written around the year 150, remind us that Jesus "came to win us by good will, for force is not of God."[11] If we want to be more effective in our ministries, I believe we will want to scrub our words of all forms of the language of obligation. If we cannot tell people why they would *want* to do something, we will make no progress in getting them to do it by telling them that we (or God) say they *should*. Ridding ourselves of the language of obligation will take some effort. We will be surprised, I think, by how frequently we lapse into it. I know I was not aware of my own habit of using words speaking of obligation, when I decided in seminary that no shoulds or oughts would pass my lips in preaching or teaching.

The language of obligation is usually shorthand for the language of desire. Even the memorably threatening, "No wire hangers!" can be expanded to mean, "I think you want your clothes to look nice when you put them on. If that's what you want, then you won't want to use wire hangers because they can give the shoulders of your blouses an ugly crease." The fact that Joan Crawford was reportedly hitting her daughter with the hanger while shouting the phrase demonstrates that the language of obligation has a lot to do with the desire to control. We will not be able quit using the language of obligation—or even think that it's a good idea to do so—until we have dealt with our control needs.

The way to get rid of the language of obligation is to translate it into the language of desire. If the sentiment cannot be translated into the language of desire, then you should not say it that way—I mean, unless you intend and desire to make your listeners angry, you will want to say it another way.

It is not that leaders should be afraid to speak for fear of offending people who have a consumer mentality and who may shop elsewhere. Let's give the laity more credit than that. People are in church only because they are looking for an encounter and relationship with the reality of God. They want to be led well because they know they need leadership to go in the direction they want to go. People refuse to heed our language of obligation because they understand that those obligations come from us, not from God. The social order is different now. The change has been building for some time, and we have largely failed to heed it. In the early 1960s a woman went to her priest to seek counsel about her physically abusive husband. "I married you for better and for worse," the priest replied. One divorce, two rectors, and twenty-five years later, the woman returned to see if the church might be taking a different approach.

The language of obligation and control is not the exclusive purview of so-called traditionalists; progressive leaders can still be all about controlling their flocks. The mouths of both women and men easily—all too easily—form words that intend to coerce, rather than invite; no one is exempt from this tendency by reason of sex or theological perspective.

There is simply no place in a post-Christendom church for any overt or implied obligation. We can no longer turn God's free invitation and gift into a list of musts and must nots. Rather, we want to inspire, to invite, to attract, and most of all, to embody in our own lives God's fervent desire to awaken in people the desire to love God back.

This is our true heritage, not the fleshpots of the establishment that twisted our thoughts and warped our values. We can help bring the church back from the brink if we reclaim that heritage and throw away the mess of pottage for which we traded it centuries ago.

CHAPTER THREE

Our Conventional Wisdom Isn't Helping

> *Do not trust in these deceptive words:*
> *"This is the temple of the LORD,*
> *the temple of the LORD, the temple of the LORD."*
> — JEREMIAH 7:4

This chapter is devoted to challenging some aspects of the current conventional wisdom in the Episcopal Church. If we are to develop both an understanding that redevelopment is urgently necessary and more effective ways of thinking about how to rebuild the Episcopal Church, we need to examine what we have been telling ourselves about our decline.

A SYSTEM PRODUCES WHAT IT IS DESIGNED TO PRODUCE

The management consultant Edwards Deming reminds us that a system cannot understand itself. We must incorporate a view from the outside if we are to develop the understanding that change requires. Archimedes needed a place to stand away the earth in order for his lever to move it. Deming's observation that "a system produces what it is designed to produce" can help move us to that independent place. He means, as Jesus meant, that we know what kind of tree it is by the fruit it produces. If a factory consistently produces inferior products, it is not because some members of the workforce are sloppy, but because, regardless of the manuals and the slogans, management has allowed the system to become one that is *designed* to produce shoddy goods. If the church has steadily declined for half a century, it means the church has become the kind of system that produces decline. It's not that there are a few bad actors in a system that would be perfect without those individuals. The system is the problem. For the results to change, the system must change.

I do not mean just rearranging the deck chairs—or the placement of the altar or pews. The system is not the same as the structure. It's quite possible to change a system completely without changing titles, roles, or job descriptions. Making the system produce quality involves changing *how* people work, not necessarily *what* they do. We mandate certain processes by making them part of the structure, as with ordination and deployment, but the system turns out the same product—decline.

Think of two parishes with the same structure: rector, two church wardens, twelve vestry members, a director of music, an administrator, a sex-

ton, and an average Sunday attendance of 125. These are accurate descriptions of two places I know well. In one a disappointed and dispirited rector is phoning it in. The administrator's main job is to cover for him. The same cycle of hymns and anthems—and sermons—is repeated every three years; in the case of Holy Week, Easter, and Christmas, every year. The sexton does only what he is told to do, and only after he's been asked a time or two whether he has completed that particular task. Attendance is 125, but that's down 50 percent from ten years ago. A dwindling group of members tries to maintain a frantic round of fundraising activities, but it isn't just increasing age that makes them feel tired. Vestry meetings drag on for hours and the parking lot meetings even longer.

In the other parish, the rector is working hard preaching, teaching, visiting the sick, and running the institution. The administrator has offered ideas that have improved the bulletin, newsletter, and e-mail communications because the rector has asked for ideas and listened carefully in a way that inspires the administrator to think about such things when he's not at work. The director of music and rector discuss the music, taking into account both what fits with the lectionary and what motivates the congregation to sing better. The director of music knows the rector wants excellence and feels supported as she pursues it. The sexton wants the buildings to reflect the pride he takes in their appearance and somehow always seems to have just completed whatever anyone was about to ask him to do. The ECW aged out some years ago, but there's a shelter and a youth basketball program run by volunteers, a knitting group, and a community youth choir funded by a grant from a local foundation in addition to a thriving Sunday school. There are events at which everyone gets an opportunity to pitch in to raise funds for good causes. The parish had been relying on its endowment in an unsustainable way. That overspending has now stopped. Attendance is 125, and that's up 30 percent in the four years the priest has been there. Vestry meetings last ninety minutes, and people have confidence in the future.

Two congregations with two different systems, but the same church structure. The system is not the same as the structure. In most of our parishes and almost all of our dioceses the system is producing decline. We must get to a vantage point outside the system so we can understand how to change its dynamics so that the system that operates in the structure can produce different results.

Conventional wisdom, however, never has a problem with the system which is purports to understand from within. Rather, conventional wisdom is passed on in the stories we tell that allow us to live in the system by justifying and excusing the system as it is. Received wisdom, whether political, social, or ecclesiastical, is *always* an impediment to an accurate and nuanced understanding. Conventional wisdom is *always* group-think that operates in place of independent analysis. Conventional wisdom, like stereotypical thinking, has just enough truth to make parts of it plausible, but like stereotypes, group-think is intellectually lazy and inadequate. Like stereotypes, conventional wisdom is always a way of shutting out complex realities we do not want to deal with. We must therefore examine our conventional wisdom and reject those parts of it, no matter how good they make us feel, which do not help us understand our actual circumstances.

The three areas of Episcopal Church group-think I will look at in this chapter are: our claims to diversity, our assertions of valuing comprehensiveness, and our approach to talking about our decline.

THE QUESTION OF DIVERSITY

Despite what we like to say, we are not diverse in our demographic composition. The membership of the Episcopal Church is estimated to be 87 percent non-Hispanic white,[12] compared to 66 percent for the U.S. population as a whole. Certainly there are areas of the country where congregations are more ethnically diverse; indeed, without the immigration of Caribbean, and to a lesser extent African, Anglicans to the United States, the Episcopal Church would be a good bit smaller than it is. The fact remains that we are significantly older, whiter, better educated, and more affluent than the population at large. I do not mean this is how it must be, but it will not change unless we recognize where we are and take steps to do things differently.

Congratulating ourselves on our diversity does not make us diverse. A friend recently became rector of a suburban parish that bills itself as a friendly church. My friend has had to try to point out that, despite their self-understanding, they are not in fact all that welcoming. We do not become friendly by telling ourselves that we are already friendly; we become friendly by becoming aware that we *want* to be friendly and then by taking actions that will make us so. These actions will of necessity be different from our past actions. If we continue to do the same things in the same way as before, we will not get different results.

In a back-from-the-dead ministry in the 1980s and 1990s, while inviting people to the coffee hour almost every week, the rector told people that he knew they wanted to be friendly, and then over and over he told them how to overcome their reticence about introducing themselves to

people they did not know, including fellow parishioners whose names they had never learned. He told them again and again how to speak to people, not just greet them, and then introduce them to other people to whom they might easily be able to connect. People then knew how friendly they were becoming by how many strangers they approached. That congregation as a whole became markedly more welcoming and inclusive, first because the members got in touch with their desire to be friendly, and second because they were given concrete ways to achieve that desire. There was an objective measure provided with no obligation, no guilt, and no self-congratulation.

UNIFORMITY VERSUS COMPREHENSIVENESS

If we are not actually very diverse racially or economically, we are also not particularly diverse liturgically. There are, to be sure, different ways of enacting the liturgies in the Prayer Book, but precisely because they are Prayer Book services there will not in the end be all that much diversity. The differences in performance seem great to us who are in the system and have learned the minutiae, but those outside the fold still generally apprehend an "Episcopal style" that communicates itself no matter how high or low the service. As a new Episcopalian I did not experience a gulf between the Morning Prayer of the low-church parish where I was confirmed in my early twenties and the solemn high mass of St. Mary the Virgin in New York, which I attended a few months after my confirmation. Only as I became acquainted with the details and history did the differences begin to seem more significant.

A glance at history demonstrates that the desire for liturgical uniformity is in our genetic code. Cranmer's preface to the first Prayer Book makes clear that suppressing liturgical diversity throughout the entire realm was as important to him as putting the services into a language the worshipers could understand. So uniformity in worship is as much a part of the establishment of a distinctive Anglicanism as Cranmer's English. The desire for uniformity is still with us despite the lip service we pay to comprehensiveness.

Over the next 250 years the Church of England proved unable to keep the Puritans and the Methodists in the fold. The inability to retain the Methodists in particular challenges any idea that Anglicanism is notably comprehensive. They did not have the quarrels with bishops, the Prayer Book, or church order that the Puritans developed. Rather, the resistance came from the establishment and seems to have been the result of concerns about control and class, which perhaps demonstrates that a lack of demographic diversity may be related to our discomfort with real liturgical diversity.

English ecclesiastical structures that had ossified in the Middle Ages could not with agility be adapted to the demographic shifts of the Industrial Revolution. The established church's inability to respond effectively to the missionary situation thus created caused the church to lose the adherence of large parts of the population. On this side of the Atlantic the stories of the missionary efforts of the Episcopal Church on the American frontier are precious to us—James Lloyd Breck's traveling chalice and paten were an ordination gift to me—but we need to recognize that those efforts were fairly ineffective, both in terms of absolute and relative numbers. If we cannot with clear eyes analyze these parts of our history, we will not see what makes missionary activity difficult for us. If we do not understand the factors that cause the difficulties, we will not be able to figure out how to make our efforts more effective.

The manner of our introduction of the 1979 *Book of Common Prayer,* to which I am devoted, was also telling. If we were indeed so liturgically comprehensive, why could we not have defused part of the controversy and permitted use of the 1928 Prayer Book more widely? And more recently, why could the Prayer Book lectionary not have been authorized for use alongside the *Revised Common Lectionary*? There was in both instances an urge toward uniformity and coercion that went unacknowledged by the majority but which was certainly felt by those on the losing end.

Surely it is instructive that Paul, almost immediately after winning the circumcision battle at the Council of Jerusalem, and while he was visiting the churches for the purpose of acquainting them with the council's decision that circumcision is unnecessary, has Timothy circumcised out of consideration for the Jews, "for they all knew that his father was a Greek" (Acts 16:3). A church or a church leader with an establishment mentality will rarely show that kind of concern for the minority opinion.

Some bishops send out lengthy instructions about what they want to encounter when they visit parishes. Perhaps they would be better leaders and learn more about the realities of their dioceses if they followed the example of the bishop who said to a rector whose liturgical preferences he did not share, "I'll do it the way you do it."[13] Besides creating a movable bubble in which the bishop does not experience anything he or she does not like, the practice of trying to make sure the service is exactly what a bishop wants also has the effect of communicating, to the clergy anyway, the unfortunate notion that the preferences of the person in charge decide the limits of liturgical comprehensiveness.

TALKING ABOUT DECLINE

Rather than speaking the truth with responsible humility, we have developed an exculpatory rhetoric to help us deal with our continuing failure. I think these claims catch the gist of that rhetoric.

Claim 1: There's nothing we can do about it.

Claim 2: Numbers are suspect, and maybe decline is a sign of faithfulness.

Claim 3: Normal models of parish ministry are obsolete.

Claim 4: The people are to blame.

Claim 5: Management is not the priest's job.

Claim 6: We can fix it by changing the canons.

Claim 7: Process trumps leadership.

Now we will look at each of these claims in more detail.

Claim 1:
There's nothing we can do about it.

You may be in a setting where the demographics and economics really do prohibit even a tenuous survival. Some parts of the country have been losing population for a century, and some Rust Belt and rural areas have endured decades of economic depression. According to a Carsey Institute study, while 17 percent of the population lives in counties with fifty thousand inhabitants or fewer,[14] 52 percent of Episcopal congregations are located in villages or small cities with fewer than fifty thousand residents.[15] As in the Church of England during the Industrial Revolution, the locations of our congregations have not changed with the massive shifts in population during the last century. Some of these now disadvantageously placed congregations may not be viable. A small town that can no longer support a restaurant or a filling station may not be able to sustain any churches. However, if the town has churches of other denominations, why not an Episcopal parish as well?

On the other hand, I think we have at times explained our decline in terms either of outside forces we can do nothing about or of political red herrings. These explanations have kept us from considering seriously how we might be contributing to the situation by our lack of vision and leadership and by our outmoded expectations.

In our need for good leadership we are no different from other not-for-profit organizations. In an article on the troubles of opera companies around the country, *The New Yorker*'s Alex Ross could easily have been writing about the mainline churches:

> Sometimes it's a matter of geography: more than a few troubled organizations are based in downtown neighborhoods ruined by decades of decay. But leadership is an even more crucial factor. The problem cases tend to show multiple symptoms of poor management: dubious real-estate moves, ham-fisted labor relations, klutzy P.R., and, above all, a lack of artistic focus. The most precious commodity is a great manager...who can handle fussy conductors, disgruntled musicians, reactionary donors, and grumbling subscribers, imagining new audiences all the while.[16]

Demographic changes, for example, may explain why the voices of the mainline churches are now softer after the demise of the Protestant ascendancy, but such shifts do not explain the loss of membership and attendance. An increase of non-mainline Christians in the population means only that the rest of us make up a smaller percentage of the population; it does not mean it was necessary for our actual numbers to decrease.

Nor will I concede that the 1979 Prayer Book and the ordination of women, in and of themselves, caused the weakening of the Episcopal Church. The decline was underway before those changes occurred, and the fall-off has affected all the mainline churches, not just ours. Phenomena unique to one denomination cannot have caused the decline of all. Neither do the liberal politics of many mainline churches after the civil rights movement and the Vietnam War bear the entire blame. The Southern Baptists are in decline as well.

Recently I spoke to a seminarian from a diocese in an area of the country that has been losing industry and population for a generation. She did not think it was reasonable in those circumstances to expect anything other than continued decline. She saw the future as continuing to urge congregations to move to part-time clergy, and to yoke and consolidate with neighboring parishes so they could continue as long as possible. It is far from my purpose to blame people who are working in such difficult circumstances, but it is necessary to say that if our reach does not exceed our grasp, we will not extend our arms, and we will never know what we could have accomplished. The Episcopal Church needs only a tiny percentage of the population to thrive. Is it really true that there is *nothing* we can do?

If decline really is the only future we can see, then we can stop training leaders. The CDO profile list for clergy skills notwithstanding, "managing decline" is not a leadership function. Decline happens all by itself. Leadership is about helping to bring a future to birth. And without blaming that seminarian who clearly loved the church and was pained by her vision of the future, it is necessary to point out that if we adopt the position that there is truly nothing we can do, then we have made our jobs a lot easier, and we have defined a threshold of "effective ministry" that no one can fail to meet. We are firmly and snugly part of a system designed to produce decline, and we may be sure that decline is what that system will continue to produce.

I grant that parishes with glorious histories are not guaranteed a thriving future in perpetuity, and it is not my purpose to second-guess every decision that has been made to close a congregation. However, I will venture to say that, even in adverse demographic and economic circumstances, parishes do not usually close after a history of effective, far-sighted leadership. Even if you cannot see the cure for all the long-term problems your parish faces, there are things you can almost certainly do in the meantime. *However, you can do these things, first, only if you believe that the congregation has a future, and second, only if you incarnate your belief in the future in words and actions in a way others find compelling.* And although it may seem "unspiritual" or not a priority for clergy leaders, as I will explain below the first thing you will need to address head-on with a congregation that is experiencing decline is money.

- You can still increase personal giving, unless all your members are already tithing. I believe you can do this only if you practice proportional giving off the top and invite others to try it because you have found it personally transformative.

- You can stop overspending your endowment if you have one. This is very difficult, and you will almost certainly need outside assistance. (See the last bullet below.)

- You can begin to reserve for future capital needs.

- You can begin a planned giving effort to establish an endowment for the buildings. If you have been overspending the endowment, you will need to mend your ways before you ask for more money.

- You can look at the arrangements you have with those who use your space. Is their rent (and it *is* rent, not a "space-use donation") covering what it costs you to provide the space? If you are subsidizing their occupancy, is that what you intended? Can you afford it? Is that how you want to be using your money? What other initiatives are you unable to undertake because you are subsidizing this tenant?

- You can look for additional revenue sources for the operating budget, for programs, and for capital work.

- To help you think about how to move ahead, you will want to call on assistance from your diocesan office. The Episcopal Church Foundation also has many resources in these areas. Contact them at www.episcopalfoundation.org.

I have so far mentioned only financial and building issues on purpose. In most declining congregations, as we will see, money and building issues are the major sources of anxiety among the people. In order to move ahead into a future, you must deal with the major sources of anxiety so that people can begin to think about other matters. Pretending that these institutional issues are not important simply will not work. How can a small liberal arts college fulfill its educational mission if the buildings are deteriorating and the college cannot make payroll? Safe, attractive buildings and adequate cash flow *enable* ministry; they are not antithetical to ministry.

While you are making the progress you can with these matters, you may be very surprised at the possibilities you encounter. These possibilities will open up for two reasons. First, people respond to effective leadership. They will step forward when things begin to move in the right direction. Second, if you focus on these matters, you will probably begin to see opportunities that were there all the time; you did not notice them before because you were not looking for them.

In addition to the matters above, you can also:

- ℘ Look at every aspect of your buildings, signage, and practices from the point of view of a newcomer and begin to revise everything accordingly to be more hospitable.

- ℘ Raise the quality of the Sunday services, making them accessible, authentic moments when we can know God in the beauty of holiness. Strive for excellence, whatever that may mean in your context. If we are just going through the motions, chasing fads, or applauding mediocrity, we cannot be surprised that the services fail to move people's hearts.

- ℘ Offer Bible study and educational opportunities for all ages in ways that meet people's desire not to know more about religion, but to know the Lord better. It may be necessary to add that we must believe the faith we proclaim.

- ℘ Find ways appropriate to the congregation to give members a chance to be involved and transformed by serving the community and the world.

The point is that there are almost certainly things you can do to improve the situation. We are not merely the victims of social trends and past mistakes. And while we're doing our jobs, who knows? God may give us a future.

Claim 2:
Numbers are suspect, and maybe decline is a sign of faithfulness.
In the presence of a negative trend that we do not know how to counteract, we will figure out a story that makes that phenomenon less important.

Many leaders of the Episcopal Church have looked at the declining membership and attendance numbers and have decided that numbers are not as important as some think. I agree that numbers are not the entire story, but I insist that they are part of the story.

An early response to the negative trends in the church was panic. From the late 1960s through the 1970s there was a crisis of confidence, especially in urban parts of the country. The prosperous postwar optimism that had propelled the nation forward for two decades seemed to crash into a wall. Cities were beset with the effects of middle class flight, financial downturns, stagflation, pollution, energy crises, riots, drug epidemics, and social disintegration. The church's decline and these serious social and economic problems combined into a kind of apocalyptic foreboding. An account of the history of the Diocese of New York, written in 1984, notes that the future historian "will know better than we how deep was a sense of despair in the late twentieth century."[17]

I remember that the sense was quite deep. When I moved to New York in 1977 in the aftermath of the City's fiscal crisis, I heard numerous sermons that predicted the imminent demise of the Episcopal Church. Aspirants to the priesthood were told that there would soon be no compensated jobs in the church. The bishop told clergy and congregations that the days of the parish church were over, and everything would be house churches soon. The end was near, so there was no need to think of a long-range future. Parishes spent down endowments and sold rectories and other property to pay operating expenses.

Almost all of the parishes thus warned still exist, but they now regret the loss of the endowments, rectories, and other real estate. Having spent the endowment to zero, one urban parish sold a brownstone in the early 1970s for $27,000 to pay current bills. Even in the weak market following the 2008 crash, that building sold recently for two million dollars.

The future is difficult to predict, but things rarely happen as quickly or as definitively as the panicked believe they will. And no matter what, selling real estate and spending the proceeds on current expenses is always a bad idea if you think there is any kind of future for your organization.

The more common response in that economic crisis was to keep going on, paying as little attention to numbers as possible as things continued to decline. And because things could be kept going despite the decline, numbers grew even less important in the minds of many. It seemed that we could continue indefinitely—both to decline and to exist. However, after several decades of decline hundreds of parishes have learned and are learning the consequences of shrinking to the point of no longer being viable.

Not paying attention to numbers and other objective measures turns out
to be a form of denial, and that's no more a strategy than is panic.

Here is a claim I think those who want to be involved in back-from-
the-dead ministry need to believe: *It is the nature of the church to grow.* If
the church is not growing, something is missing, or something is not
healthy. I think the author of the Acts of the Apostles would agree with
me on this, but I understand how foreign, how upsetting and how threatening this sounds in the echo chamber of our conventional wisdom after
decades of decline.

Here again I think we can usefully make the act of translation to look
at ourselves from a different point of view. No county historical society
can continue to run budget deficits every year, overspend its endowment,
allow its building to crumble, stop asking people to renew their membership, and expect to go on indefinitely. Healthy, well-led organizations grow.
That's what they do. If that's not what your parish is doing, it's worth
thinking about why. Get an outside voice to help you think this through
so you and the rest of the leadership do not let yourselves off the hook too
easily. If in your community there is any not-for-profit dependent on private funding that is doing well, then there is no objective reason your parish
cannot also do well.

One adaptation to our situation is to see virtue in decline. Maybe you've
heard someone say, "Jesus told us to feed the sheep, not to count them,"
although the parable of the ninety-and-nine indicates that the shepherd
knows exactly how many sheep there are and where they are. Embattled
and disheartened leaders can see decline as a mark of purity and righteous-
ness. "Sure," a priest told a colleague whose congregation was growing,
"you can do things that get people to come, but is that the gospel?" Is "the
old, old story of Jesus and his love" that repellent to all but the saving remnant?

On the other hand, the Episcopal Church has never represented more
than a tiny remnant of the total population. At the height of its prestige
the Episcopal Church was about one percent of the population.[18] Today
the average Sunday attendance of the Episcopal Church is about a quarter
of one percent of a population of three hundred million. Would we really
have to sell out the gospel completely to have one-half or three-quarters of
one percent in attendance?

Numbers matter because *it is not possible to continue to decline and to
continue to exist.* Membership, attendance, income, resources for building
maintenance—these numbers matter in the same ways and to the same
extent that the equivalent numbers matter for opera companies, colleges,

museums, hospitals, and other not-for-profits with a mission. The economist Herbert Stein noted, "Unsustainable trends tend not to be sustained." Many of our congregations are experiencing unsustainable trends with regard to attendance, finances, and building maintenance. In many cases I am convinced that effective, future-oriented leadership and work can reverse the unsustainable trend. Without that leadership, however, the trend will not be sustained because the parish will close.

Claim 3:
Normal models of parish ministry are obsolete.
For centuries in the church the normal model of parish ministry has been one ordained person leading a congregation, assisted by whatever ordained and lay staff the parish can afford. The one priest, one parish model is not only what has been normal; it is also what people like and expect. It has also been more effective and more sustainable than any other model of which I am aware. Of course the model has never been universal. Two or more small rural congregations have often been served by a single priest. Now, after decades of decline, more and more historically self-sustaining parishes have found it increasingly difficult to fund the traditional model.

This has led to something of an industry of (mostly) clergy trying to convince laypeople that the model is obsolete and that moreover it was never all that good anyway. What we need, they say, are innovative models. The "innovations" always consist of one priest serving more than one congregation, either by yoking two together or by having three priests cover five congregations or some other configuration.

If you ask the laypeople of congregations that are exploring these "innovative" models whether they would consider this option if they had enough money to fund their own full-time priest, they will of course say no. To tell the people that they are wrong to want to continue the model of priestly presence they have had since the parish was founded requires a certain amount of contempt for the laity, but many clergy and diocesan leaders are up to that job. We will note frequently the tendency of clergy to blame the laity for what are really leadership failures.

In fact, there is no innovation here. All these models of yoked and shared ministry have historical precedents. The difference is that in the past most people in such situations were in new missions that were looking forward to the time when the congregation would be a self-supporting parish with its own rector. Now we are simply acquiescing to decline (almost always without any kind of plan to reverse the decline), but we are trying to cloak that by applying theological lipstick to an economic pig.

In one diocese in a metropolitan area, two nearby congregations that had been in decline for some time embarked on conversations to see if some kind of consolidation made sense. The clergy and the diocesan office said they were discussing mission strategy, but when asked, the laypeople of both parishes said they would not be having these discussions if they had enough money. I told the parishes that it was worth trying to address the chronic underfunding of each parish, since neither was that far from financial health, and I could see things that might be able to be done to achieve that health. I said that if it made sense strategically to share resources and to consolidate efforts in areas of ministry, it would still be a strategically sound decision to do so even if money were not a problem.

The model of parish ministry we have had for centuries is not obsolete; it is simply more challenging to fund. If it is necessary to retrench, either temporarily or for the foreseeable future, so be it, but let's use the language that most accurately describes the situation. Acquiescing to decline is neither an innovation nor a strategy.

Claim 4:
The people are to blame.
If you are immersed in the conventional wisdom that justifies our decline, you may not be aware of the extent to which that justification lays the blame on the people. The people aren't committed. The people aren't generous. The people act like consumers. The people are resisting what needs to happen. The people are priest-killers. Blaming the people is a necessary part of the lore that makes the ordained leaders of a declining church feel better.

Of course it's not true. At least it's not true in the way the leadership would like it to be true. Here's an example of what I mean. Most appeals for pledges and fundraising in the church consist of leaders saying that the church needs the people's money in order to pay bills and to continue in existence, and the appeals come wrapped in the idea that everyone is under some kind of obligation to contribute more, and that by not upping their pledge they are resisting "what God is calling us to do." When people do not respond to such off-putting techniques, we blame them for not supporting the church. The fact is that the leadership has not asked rightly. It is possible to talk about money in ways that empower people to be as generous as they have always wanted to be. Talk that communicates anxiety, obligation, and guilt will not work. The problem is not people who do not respond to such language; the problem is leadership that uses that kind of language.

It is simply not the case that the people are supposed to respond with money, dedication, and good cheer no matter what kind of leadership they have. It would be easier for us if that were the case, but we cannot abdicate our responsibilities that way. Almost everything we blame the laypeople for—including the scarcity of laypeople in many parishes—is actually a result of poor leadership.

As we will see, one of the points of this book is that effective leaders see the people as the solution, not as the problem. Yes, there are individuals who can be particularly obnoxious, but in every declining parish I know, it is not necessary to get rid of problematic individuals; rather, it is necessary to begin to make the system healthier. Then the people in the system will get healthier. If the obnoxious people do not join in the process of getting healthier as everybody else does, they will sideline themselves, because the rest of the congregation will prefer health to dysfunction.

Communities of faith, like every organization, respond to leadership. It contradicts our conventional wisdom, but observation and experience have taught me that the people in both declining and reviving parishes are faithful; parishes decline under ineffective leadership and revive when there is good leadership.

Claim 5:
Management is not the priest's job.
During the same years that much has been said and written about empowering lay ministry, the church has actually become more clericalized. In the days of the 1928 Prayer Book, before the Eucharist was widely accepted as the principal act of worship on the Lord's Day, the presence of a priest every Sunday in every church was not essential, since many small congregations had lay readers trained to lead Morning Prayer. Now a great deal of effort is expended in securing the services of supply priests. A freestanding altar makes the priest's facial expressions and gestures more of a focal point, especially when the celebrant now often sits behind the altar, facing the congregation. Eucharistic vestments also make the priest more distinctive than did a tippet or stole over the same cassock and surplice that choir members and acolytes wore. And in my lifetime "Mister" and "Doctor," forms of address shared by laypeople, have disappeared as ways to address clergy.

My preferences are old-fashioned Anglo-Catholic, so of these developments I bemoan only the freestanding altar, but I think the effects of all of them need to be pointed out and taken into consideration.

It may not be coincidental that during a period of clericalization and decline, clergy seem more and more to feel that the leadership of the institution is the laity's job. It was always the role of the vestry as the parish corporation to oversee the assets of the parish, including finances, but as the finances become more and more difficult to deal with, I see a tendency among many clergy to try to edit any concern for these matters completely out of their job description.

It will not work. Clergy in charge of congregations are in most ways like the executive directors of not-for-profits. It is always the executive director's job to manage the institutional life of the organization, which includes both the programs that are the mission of the organization and the money, staff, volunteers, and buildings that enable the programs to take place. Boards are not good at management; their proper role is governance.

At a recent vestry retreat I led, I asked those present to recount their most satisfying and their most frustrating moments of vestry service. This parish has had a series of rectors who stayed five to eight years with a typical gap of eighteen to twenty-four months between incumbents. I was not sure where things would go, but I was not surprised when it turned out that people uniformly had found it frustrating when the vestry was in the position of having to manage the operation. Decisions were difficult to make, and when they were finally made, months went by before they were implemented. The experiences the members had found satisfying were those moments when they could make policy or financial decisions based on information and recommendations from committees or the rector and know that their decisions would be acted on by the staff.

Members of the vestry may be among the volunteer staff that manages things under the supervision of the rector, but when the vestry meets, the discussion should be about governance. Let the management decisions be made at regular meetings of the paid and unpaid staff chaired by the priest.

Claim 6:
We can fix it by changing the canons.
In the messy aftermath of the 2010 ecclesiastical court decision that reinstated the Bishop of Pennsylvania after an inhibition and lengthy proceedings, there was much internet discussion about changing the canons to provide for dioceses and their bishops the equivalent of the dissolution of the pastoral relationship between a rector and vestry. I agree that the considerations that led to the changes in life tenure for rectors are at least as urgent for bishops. It is simply unhealthy for people not to need to be ac-

countable to those they lead. However, we must remember that structural solutions do not fix systemic problems.

Our problems are systemic. That is, they have to do with how we act within our structures. Systems do not become healthier or more effective by changing the structure in which the system operates. Edwin Friedman's writings, as far as I can tell, always discourage structural change as a way of improving the functioning of the system. We do not need to reorganize or change titles or job descriptions to get an office to work better. Rather, we need leadership that listens and allows and encourages people to give their best. It is a fact that numerous parishes and more than a few dioceses have chosen manifestly inappropriate leaders. Structural changes will not address this situation. And yet this is the situation that needs to be addressed if we want the church to be turned around.

Claim 7:
Process trumps leadership.
In the 1990s two cardinal parishes in one diocese called new rectors while the incumbents were still in place. There was no interim priest, parish profile, or any other part of the "normal" transition process, as we now call it. At a clergy conference soon after, a priest asked the bishop why they had been allowed to do that when other parishes had to go through the usual procedures that took up to two years. Proving Michael Kinsley's maxim that a gaffe is just truth slipping out, the bishop replied with jaw-dropping candor, "Those are important institutions that can't have a break in leadership."

Well-led and well-run not-for-profits try not to have a long hiatus between executive directors. The boards of important institutions know that it would be irresponsible not to do succession planning. Important institutions know they cannot have a break in leadership because they know leadership is important.

Think about our conventional wisdom with regard to clergy transitions. The shocking aspect of the way we now call clergy is precisely that we agree with the candid bishop's implication about most parishes. We do not believe that parishes are important institutions that need good leadership in order to thrive. If we thought that parishes were important and that effective leadership was important to their health and growth, we would not use the system we have been using.

The longer a parish has been without adequate leadership, the less likely it is that the parish will be able successfully to complete the call process. And the fact that most vestries and clergy find the system frustrating and unsatisfactory begs the question: whose interests are served by continuing the current system?

Certainly the current system for calling clergy does not serve the interests of parishes like the one whose vestry retreat I conducted. For almost forty years that congregation has been a textbook example of how our conventional wisdom thinks things should be done. It is a typical pastoral congregation with a modest plant and no endowment. The rectors have stayed five to eight years, and they have gone through the full interim process every time. They have always had competent, hardworking, sometimes visionary rectors. By the time each rector leaves, the parish is almost back to the point where it was when the previous rector resigned. Proving the candid bishop correct, the parish has been weakened by each interim period—not by bad interims, though several were cavalier and lazy, but because the parish has lacked settled leadership one year out of four. The lay leadership is well aware of this reality. They know this is not the way to run a railroad.

I am not aware that clergy generally feel that the current system serves their interests either. The system was devised in part to break open the "old boys' network," through which positions were dispensed by the bishop, and it has largely succeeded in that. On the other hand, it can easily take years for a priest to find a new job, and because the system encourages people to call and be called according to a profile that may or may not be accurate, bad matches are hardly unknown. Search committees frequently do not communicate well, and unfortunate things can occur at diocesan offices.

A dispassionate analysis would indicate that the principal effect of the current system has been to reduce the level of responsibility of the bishop's office, both to the congregations and to the clergy. Though of course a bishop's favorites still get preferment, in general there is no vocational development in the Episcopal Church. If you think you're ready for a new job, go get one. And I have seen plenty of dissolutions of the pastoral relationship where the bishop felt no particular responsibility because, after all, he had let the parish call the priest they wanted.

The inescapable conclusion is that the assumptions underlying our current systems for clergy deployment and leadership are along these lines:

   ❧ Parish priests are ineffective and dysfunctional. Therefore it is necessary to have a period of healing after each one leaves. The longer the priest was there, the more healing will be necessary.

§ We cannot allow succession planning to happen while the incumbent is still in place, because that person will meddle and interfere in ways detrimental to the parish, thus proving the truth of the previous bullet that parish priests do not have the best interests of the parish at heart.

§ Effective, sustained leadership is not as important as process. Therefore it isn't a problem if the interim period continues for several years.

§ Bishops cannot be trusted. Therefore we need something as close to an open-call system as possible.

§ The pastoral relationship is shallow and less important than proper process. Therefore the people are rightly directed not to want the priest who ministered to them and their families for years to conduct a loved one's funeral or baptize their child during an interim period, or at any point after that priest's departure, depending on today's definition of proper process.

In other words, our procedures have been devised in order to manage around dysfunctional priests and untrustworthy bishops. The solution does not lie in that direction; such a reactive system is designed to produce decline. Every organization has a vital interest in making sure that each of its local sites is a worthy and thriving embodiment of the organization. And to that end, every sensible organization knows that the leaders of those locations are important assets that need to be groomed, developed, supported, and replaced quickly when they move on.

There seems to be the beginnings of an understanding on the part of some dioceses that what we have been doing does not work well. I applaud any efforts to try to move how we handle deployment in a more rational direction.

Let's understand that the candid bishop was right about those two cardinal parishes, but let's extend his wisdom to all our parishes. First, all parishes are important, and second, leadership is important for every parish. If that's what we come to believe—and we must come to believe it, for our procedures demonstrate that we do not believe that now—we will want to change our procedures to reflect that belief. Whatever procedures we use to fill leadership positions need to be in strict service to the two truths that 1) parishes are important and 2) leadership is important. If the process has some other agenda or some other assumptions, the parishes and the clergy—and therefore the entire church—will suffer.

Conventional wisdom is a hindrance to clear thinking. We need to clear our minds of our group-think so that we can see our real situation and its actual possibilities. Let's consider now what happens when you get your turnaround opportunity.

CHAPTER FOUR

Packing Your Toolkit

*I appeal to you therefore, brothers and sisters, by the mercies of God,
to present your bodies as a living sacrifice, holy and acceptable to
God, which is your spiritual worship. Do not be conformed
to this world, but be transformed by the renewing of
your minds, so that you may discern what is the will
of God—what is good and acceptable and perfect.*
— ROMANS 12:1–2

This chapter will focus on the attitude, style, and spirit leaders need to bring with them into a back-from-the-brink situation. Here I concentrate on aspects of the interior work that is an essential part of the method I have found to be effective in turning parishes around. In the next chapter we will discuss how to get started once a leader arrives.

I am trying to be as specific as possible about this interior work, which focuses not on what to do, but on what kind of person you need to have become, what attitudes and style you need to project in order to bring a parish back from the dead, or near death. How do we need to *be* in the situation, in order to see its possibilities and begin to bring them to life? In this work we are not given a list of things that need to be done or par-

ticular ways of doing them. Rather, we need to be enlivened by the right
kind of spirit as we approach this task. That spirit and approach will allow
us to be effective both in recognizing what needs to be done and in doing
those things in an effective way. In this chapter we will look at a number
of specific attitudes that support the work of leading a congregation that
has arrived at the brink and needs to be turned around.

MAKE ALL RELATIONSHIPS TWO-WAY

You will not be effective unless you practice mutual accountability in all
your relationships with the members and leaders of the parish. Mutual accountability is a rare commodity in the church today. People at every level
regularly try to make themselves unaccountable to those they lead. There
are rectors who cow their vestries, lay leaders who have a death grip on
some aspect of parish life, and bishops who make it clear they do not wish
to hear the truth and punish those who speak up.

The only way you can lead effectively is to make all your relationships
in the congregation two-way relationships. Make yourself approachable,
so that those you lead can tell you their truth. Especially if you are in a situation that is on the brink, there is no place for defensiveness or nice dis-
tinctions of position. You need to hear the truth; otherwise your judgments
will be skewed. You are taking over as the captain of a ship that is in real
trouble. The focus has to be entirely on the work that needs to be done to
repair and strengthen the vessel and to chart a new course. Rank and recognition just do not matter. You need to model the kind of approach that
pays no attention to slights or intemperate remarks but rather concentrates
on the work at hand. I believe that rank and recognition do not matter in
any church situation, but especially in a turnaround situation you will simply sabotage any chance of success if you continue to play the normal
games that result from thinking it's all about you. It's not about you.

Since the congregation has probably arrived at this situation because of
past failures in leadership, there will very likely be no trust in the failing
system you are taking over. Maintaining relationships of mutual accountability is the only way to begin to rebuild that trust. Here are some quick
tips to keep yourself strictly accountable.[19]

   ❧ If parishioners want to give you a title, give them a title when
      you address them. Call by their first names without a title only
      those people who call you by your first name without a title.

❧ Insist on paying your way. Don't accept a complimentary ticket to a fundraising dinner or Shrove Tuesday pancake supper. Wait in the buffet line if the people will let you. On the other hand, if the dinner organizers really want to serve you and have you sit at a head table, acquiescing graciously to their desire is a better form of leadership than insisting on your own way.

Greetings, my Lord, most eminent rector and really holy person.

And to you, my Lord, most eminent usher and really holy person.

❧ Don't ask anyone to do anything you aren't willing to do. Be, and be seen to be, an equal partner in the work.

❧ Being right is less important than being trusted, so don't always insist on your points. Choose very carefully the ditches you need to defend: there are not as many as you might think. Be patient. You'll get another crack at that situation.

❧ Don't get defensive when you are criticized. Understand that most of the time it's the system talking, not just an individual. It's not personal. Acting out of defensiveness is *always* a mistake. And failing to recognize your defensiveness as defensiveness is a serious impediment to effective work.

❧ Be aware of any times you begin to feel entitled to certain treatment, to deference, to trust, or to anything at all. Feelings of any kind of entitlement are a sign that you are moving into one-way, unaccountable relationships.

❧ Never suggest that a person who is a problem for you should resign from the vestry or leave the parish.

Everything hinges on your willingness to be truly accountable to those you lead, to build relationships that are truly mutual. This is literally the *sine qua non* of good leadership; without this kind of mutuality your leadership will simply not be effective. The turnaround liturgy will not have the right spirit, and it just won't work.

It is important not to deceive yourself on this point—and there are so many ways we gladly deceive ourselves in this matter. "I view myself as a servant leader," a priest said to justify her practice of ignoring a rubric in order to do a part of the liturgy according to her personal theological preferences. There is quite a bit of self-deception here. In the first place, servants do not set the terms of their service. Servants do not write their own job descriptions, select the duties they will perform, and decide on the manner in which they will perform them. If you have the option of telling others what parts of the job you will do and how you are going to do them, then you not only are not a servant, but you are also not acting like one. And servants do not have the luxury of blowing off the rules they do not like. Nothing is going to go very well if we can say we are servants when we do not hold ourselves accountable even to the rubrics of the Prayer Book.

Here's a mental habit that can help. Be deeply aware that every decision you make could be wrong. If it bothers you that you cannot be certain you are right, you have got some work to do before you are ready to lead any kind of organization. Although you need to be prepared to give an orderly account at all times of why you're doing what you're doing and why you're doing it the way you're doing it, you must also accept the fact that there could be a better way. Bear in mind that there is no one right way to do anything. Let that sink in: *there is no one right way to do anything.*

If you change something in the liturgy, for example, make sure there is a good reason that does not have to do with your personal preferences. This includes the changes that you say are based on your theology. Citing a theological rationale for changing the liturgy is usually just an attempt to put a gloss on your preferences in a way intended to shut down disagreement. The liturgy belongs to the people, not to the priest. Don't mess with it unless there is a compelling strategic reason to do so.

Here's a small example of what I mean by a strategic reason for a liturgical change. At one parish I served the custom was for the clergy to reenter the sanctuary after the postlude to consume the elements and do the ablutions. I changed this practice on my first Sunday, not because there is a "right" place or way to do the ablutions, but because the clergy had previously held themselves aloof from the people, and this custom prevented them from interacting with the people immediately after the service. I wanted to be free to greet visitors at the door, and to make myself available for conversations with parishioners who wished to speak with a member of the clergy.

Before you arrive, you need to have the firm, conscious intention to make all of your relationships truly mutually accountable.

BELIEVE THAT DEATH
IS NOT INEVITABLE

If the place is going to be turned around, you also need to bring with you into the situation some idea that death is not inevitable. You need some idea of how things could be different. If you cannot see some new possibilities in the situation, and if you do not have a couple of ideas about ways those possibilities can be explored, you are probably not the one who can lead a turnaround.

Many times these ideas will need to come from you. It is likely that the people left in the congregation will be too distracted, sad, and angry to be able to articulate much of a constructive vision. Their energies will have been mostly devoted just to keeping the thing going another year, another month, another week.

There will almost certainly be a lot of conflict among those who remain in the congregation. They will probably be angry at those they blame for the situation in which they find themselves—past clergy and usually the past or current leadership of the diocese. In most instances their anger will be justified. Almost certainly the congregation has reached this sad state because of bad leadership, and quite often for whatever reason the bishop did nothing to help.

Let's translate this for a moment into a secular situation. Can you imagine a regional director of a franchise operation who would permit a branch manager to run an IHOP or McDonald's into the ground over a period of decades? Would the Girl Scouts permit a terrible leader to ruin the brand for a generation? I have seen really bad situations in a congregation or diocese allowed to persist for decades. Everyone sees what is going on, but nobody does anything. If action is taken, it is brutal and not consistent with similar situations and therefore strengthens the conviction of clergy and congregations that bishops should not be given much power. In general the suspicious mistrust with which diocesan offices are regarded has been earned, although this does not mean that bishops and diocesan staff lacked good intentions.

Here's where our willful disregard of objective measures comes back to bite us. Over time, the effects of the lack of mutual accountability in our system have become more and more difficult to reverse. A primary assertion of this book is that the right kind of priestly leadership is essential in bringing a congregation back from the brink. Those turnarounds generally cannot happen without episcopal leadership from bishops whose actions demonstrate genuine concern both for the vocational satisfaction and health of the clergy and for the importance and continued viability of the congregations they lead. In dioceses that have that kind of leadership, enterprising clergy will find the support they need to lead congregations back from the dead.

Let's hope you have that kind of support. If you do not find help coming from the diocesan office, try to find it among any other clergy who are working to turn places around. Keep your eyes and ears open for new ideas as you share experiences with these other clergy and as you read. You'll need a steady supply of ideas to try because a good many of them won't stick.

Remember, you're changing the system, not necessarily the structure. In commenting on the turnaround at a large, failing public high school in Brockton, Massachusetts, the state's education commissioner David Driscoll said, "In schools, no matter the size—and Brockton is one of the biggest—what matters is uniting people behind a common purpose, setting high expectations, and sticking with it."[20] That's a pretty good description of the job no matter what kind of organization you are turning around, with the caveat that the high expectations cannot be one-way. If you have high expectations of others, make sure they have high expectations of you, and make sure you are accountable to them.

BE ENCHANTED

Encourage yourself to be smitten with the place. You need to love it. No matter what shape they are in or how inadequate they are, you need to love the buildings. No matter how difficult some of the people may be, you need to love the congregation. You need to love the congregation's possibilities no matter how clearly you see its problems.

A bishop asked a friend who has done this work in three parishes, "What makes you so effective?" My friend responded, "I don't want to sound like a greeting card, but it's all about love."

This affection, I hope, comes in part unbidden, but you need to help yourself fall in love with the congregation. One way is to identify completely with the place. Never say "they" in referring to the parish. A colleague spent about ten years in a marginal parish. She is competent and hard-working, and the parishioners liked and respected her. She had to resign finally because they simply could no longer afford to pay her. I feel sure that part of the reason her work was not effective was that she always referred to the parish in the third person. Not once did I ever hear her say "we're doing" or "we're trying." It was always "they." And in speaking to the vestry or congregation it was always "you," never "we." Her speech expressed how she felt. That lack of identification communicated itself and, I believe, undermined her work.

Take a generous view of the congregation's history. There will have been some missteps and some bad actors, but you need to identify with the parish's history the way you do with your own family's history. One parish had relocated two miles inland when their once-residential coastal location had become a desolate industrial waterfront with no parking. Forty years later a new rector said publicly he hoped that, if the parish's current neigh-

borhood changed, they would not "abandon" it. The statement misread the motives of those who had made the decision and overlooked the fact that the move was a judicious placement of an Episcopal parish in a developing area that needed one.

Another way to help yourself fall in love is to get completely familiar with every part of the buildings. Without denying their problems, look at them through eyes that see them both as what they are and as what they can be. My partner and I have restored two Victorian houses that were in terrible shape when we bought them. It was more than twenty years before we could undertake the exterior restoration of the second one. All that time when I looked at the house, I saw the phony-brick asphalt shingles that *were* there, but I also saw the new cedar clapboard and the combination of colors that I knew one day *would be,* and now are, there.

Examine your relationship with the buildings. Are you occupying and using them without connecting with them? When my mother sold the house she owned for over thirty years, she said it was difficult, not because the house was anything so special, but because she had cleaned, washed, painted, and papered every square inch of it again and again. That's the kind of connection I mean. Even if your hope is one day to replace the decrepit parish house with a new building, it's important to love with your body whatever buildings you have in whatever shape they are.

I do not wish to sound like a greeting card at all. This love is not easy. A parish at the brink of failure will be a brutally fractious place. You will occasionally be hit by a missile one member was aiming at another. Sometimes the bombs will be aimed at you. People will frequently act in unlovable ways. Falling plaster and leaky foundations do not inspire affection. This love will often need to be a matter of the will, not of warm fuzzy feelings.

You are taking on an incredibly difficult task. If you succeed, people will describe your tenure as a magic time. There's no unchristian fascination with the occult in that; they mean that as they look back, they see what happened as gratuitous, unearned, something beyond a reductive explanation of cause and effect. The priests I have spoken to who have successfully done this work express an affection for the parish that they somewhat self-consciously acknowledge is a bit foolish. I am convinced that this kind of unreasonable love is a necessary part of a successful turnaround.

KEEP SOME EMOTIONAL PERSPECTIVE

You need to love the place, but you also need some emotional and intellectual perspective. I'm talking about something more than self-care, like taking your days off and spending an appropriate amount of time with your family. We need time away from our work, but I think we need ways of processing our work that help us keep things in perspective. It is far too easy to be tripped up by our own baggage, overwhelmed by the interpersonal conflict, or sucked into the dysfunction. Here are three suggestions for ways to prevent this from happening.

First, there are mental games you can cultivate that protect you from immediate negative emotional reactions. For example, if a parishioner can be counted on to say the same kind of annoying thing every time you speak with him or her, you might try something like this. When I was born, my father was the pastor of an American Baptist church near New Haven,

Connecticut. His parents would drive up from Atlantic City, New Jersey, to visit. My grandfather, having ascertained to his satisfaction that my mother was taking good care of my father, would always say to my grandmother, "Well, Margaret, we can go home now." My mother, unsure of her place in a family very different from her family of origin, always took the remark as a criticism and felt hurt. After a while she decided that, since the remark was sure to come, she would make a bet with herself about whether he would say it ten minutes into the visit or seven or five. She found that the negative impact of my grandfather's remark was blunted because instead of focusing on the remark, she could congratulate herself for guessing correctly or she could analyze why he had said it before or after the time she had predicted. Such a tactic works better than simply counting to ten, because it gives your mind something to work on that is related to the situation, and thus gives you the distance you need to regain your perspective.

As headmaster of several private schools, a friend of mine took the minutes of trustee meetings. He told me that, to help him deal with his frustrations with the board, for three months running he wrote the minutes in advance of the meetings and found he did not have to change anything.

Writing the script in advance and anticipating negativity can help us keep our heads cool in some situations, but more is needed. If we were therapists or psychologists, we would be in supervision. We would need to speak of our interactions with individuals and committees, much as we did while discussing verbatims during the Clinical Pastoral Education we took. Someone would be asking us why we said what we said, why we did what we did. Such conversations would also help give us some emotional perspective that we could take back into our work. I am not suggesting that such sessions be required; our system is still far too reactive to introduce yet one more required venue for one-way relationships. Peer groups can work just as well, if the members of the group keep themselves accountable to one another.

If you are leading a back-from-the-brink situation, I hope you have one or two colleagues you can meet with or at least call regularly. Try to find such a person if you do not have one. It needs to be someone with whom you can share failures as well as successes, so you will need to be careful to find someone you can trust as well as someone with whom you are compatible. In my observation and experience, clergy gatherings or deanery meetings probably will not serve this purpose. Such gatherings, useful as they are for staying connected, just are not the right setting for the kind of conversations I'm talking about here.

There are other exercises that might help. In all the time I have been in turnaround situations, I have been writing books that have been directly related to my work. This has forced me to put my efforts into perspective, because I have had to organize my impressions and think about what other eyes would see in what I write. Keeping a journal may also serve the purpose, if there is someone else you can share it with.

I think the point is to find some way of processing your experiences in the presence of someone who is trustworthy and supportive, but who will not just give you a pass. This is not easy, and I cannot pretend I have always done this well. This job may break you, as I have been broken. When your strength fails, I hope you have a loving spouse or partner, some good friends, and a bishop who understands. I am lucky in my current situation to have all three.

REMEMBER: LAYPEOPLE ARE THE SOLUTION, NOT THE PROBLEM

If you have not yet cleared your mind of all traces of our unhelpful conventional wisdom, you may have the idea that dysfunctional or even priest-killing laypeople have brought the parish to the brink. This is almost certainly false. The parish is on its knees because of past leadership failures. If people are dysfunctional, it is because they have been part of a system designed to produce dysfunction. They had to cover for the rector, or they had to pick up the pieces of his job that he wasn't doing, or they had to fight the priest's desire to overspend the endowment or be unaccountable. They saw things falling apart and did what they could to hold things together. Leadership shapes the system, and the system forms the people who are part of it. Bad leadership makes a dysfunctional system, and such a system twists the people that are part of it.

In the three turnaround situations I have led, I have found even in the difficult people a deep faith, a realistic awareness of previous mistakes, and an urgent longing for the parish to be healthy and to thrive. There are always controlling people who are playing inappropriate roles in the life of the parish, but there are good reasons for that. They probably *needed* to play those roles to ensure the survival of the parish. They have power and influence in the system because they kept the entire thing from tanking, and other people know that, even if they do not like everything the controlling people are doing. The people in those roles will of course resist your efforts to make the system healthier; it is difficult for people to move

from survival mode to growth mode, particularly if such a change will diminish their power.

We will discuss this more in depth in chapter 8, which is devoted to
interpersonal relationships. The point here is that you need to bring with
you a deep respect for the laypeople of the parish. You need to connect
with their desire to make things better. That desire is there, and if you un-
leash it, tremendous things can happen. The laypeople who have remained
in a failing situation are not the problem; they are part of the solution.

INTEGRATE YOUR PRAYER
AND YOUR WORK

It is not my purpose to suggest a particular kind of devotional practice,
other than to say that it is necessary to have one that suits you. My intent
in this section is to make some points about prayer that I think are particularly helpful to people leading a turnaround situation.

W. H. Auden wrote, "To pray is to pay attention or, shall we say, to 'listen' to someone or something other than oneself." In most situations we
do not really listen to voices other than our own. We hear enough to know
if opposition to our point of view is being expressed. If so, we turn our efforts to persuading or neutralizing or excluding that opposition. I want to
suggest that, especially in the conflict you will find in parishes at the brink
of failure, we need to listen more carefully to the voices that are not our
own.

It is helpful to see the wisdom of the Benedictine expression "to work
is to pray." There is no disjunction between our prayer and our work. Our
study, meditation, and contemplation are not pit stops that halt the journey
temporarily. Rather, they are part of the road, as are our days of rest and
relaxation. All aspects of our work—dealing with architects and contractors, visiting with parishioners, speaking with those who come by for help,
trying to get meaningful financial reports prepared for the vestry, inspiring
and thanking the staff, developing outreach programs, thinking about ways
to make the budget healthier, talking about ways to welcome visitors more
effectively, and everything else—are our prayer. The old hymn says, "Prayer
is the soul's sincere desire."[21] If your soul's sincere and central desire is for
the future good of the place you are serving, your work may tire and frus-
trate you, but even the stressful and weird parts will often exhilarate and
satisfy.

Seeing your work as part of your spiritual life, because you understand
that truly listening to those who disagree with you is part of your prayer,

allows you to see God's hand in what you are doing. When I think about how exactly the right person would come forward to join the staff just when we needed those particular skills, or how situations that could have been toxic developed instead into moments of healing, even in retrospect tears well in my eyes. At the time experiences like these were spiritually rich for me, and they were also steps forward for the parish.

We deceive ourselves if we think our prayer life is unrelated to our work because the proof of our spiritual formation is how we do our work. In one diocese the chair of the Commission on Ministry spoke to new clergy of the hours she spent every day in meditation. It sounded amazing and made us all feel inadequate. However, she bullied the succession of curates she employed, and during her tenure there spent three-quarters of the principal of the endowment, jumping to a more prestigious parish just before things started to get really bad. I recommend a spiritual practice that keeps you firmly in touch with what is best for the parish you are serving.

Burnout is not caused by working hard or working in a difficult job. Burnout is the result of working in a place we do not like, of working at something we are not very good at, or of overfunctioning in our job. Overfunctioning is either concerning ourselves with things that aren't our job, or failing to let situations ripen so we can see what God might do. If you are doing what you love, and you are doing it in a place and with people you love, and you know you need to wait for the latter rain as well as the early rain, and, very importantly, if you have a bishop who cares about the health of the clergy and of the parishes, you will work hard, you may often feel stressed, but I doubt you will burn out.

Ask for the prayers of others, for the parish, for your work, and for yourself. This was one of the ways my experience at Intercession changed me. Like many clergy, I am a Type A caregiver. I am the responsible one; I will take care of what you need. No thanks, I don't need anything; I'm doing fine. When the bishop asked me to take on Intercession, I was already working too many hours, and the strain was tremendous. I found great comfort and release in acknowledging for the first time my need for the prayers of others, and the wise and devoted people of Intercession, as well as other kind colleagues and friends, constantly reminded me that both the future of the parish and I were in their prayers. I am convinced that I would have failed had I not acknowledged my need, and had there not been a great cloud of witnesses praying for what we were all doing together.

LET PROPORTIONAL GIVING
CHANGE YOU

In my observation and experience nothing changes us the way tithing changes us, and those who do not give generously and proportionally will find it difficult to approach the turnaround liturgy with the attitude and spirit that will make it effective. I do not mean that because tithing is a practice enjoined on us by Scripture and General Convention resolutions, we have to follow these rules in order to be effective. No, I mean that tithing transforms our relationship with money, and we cannot deal with the financial problems of a turnaround situation if our relationship with money has not undergone that transformation.

Money is the most important sign in our lives because, as Jesus said, "Where your treasure is, there will your heart be also." If Jesus is right, then our hearts follow our money, so changing how we use our money will work a change in our hearts; we are body-selves. Changing the physical pattern of what we give and how we give it is the indispensable first step. In the discussion that follows I will use "tithing" and "proportional giving off the top" interchangeably. I believe the crux is not the percentage we give, but the fact that we give some percentage off the top before we do anything else.

If we pledge a certain number of dollars every week or every month, that number has some arbitrary aspects. Maybe there was a number we chose years ago, and we have raised it from time to time. If we give so many dollars a week, we probably do not calculate the amount as a percentage of our income, and the pattern of our giving is unrelated to when we get paid and how much we receive. We have calculated to pay the church an amount we think we can afford.

In other words, it is a number very much like the numbers on all the bills we pay. We do not decide what others charge us for the goods and services we consume. We decide whether we will pay what they ask, and we may shop around, but in the end if we want a cell phone, we will pay the going rate. By pledging to give the church a certain dollar amount we think we can afford, like buying the television service we can afford, and by paying off that obligation on a schedule not related to when we receive money, we turn the experience of giving to the church into an experience that is exactly like that of paying the phone bill or the gas bill. There's a number we have agreed to pay, and now we must pay it when it is due. No matter what we try to tell ourselves about what we are giving the church, it will feel like we are paying a bill because we have made the experience of supporting the church into the experience of paying a bill.

Proportional giving off the top has a different effect because it is a different experience. What we give varies from week to week, based first on the percentage we have decided to give, and second on whether we have received any money since the previous Sunday. If we get all our money once a month, we will make our gift on the following Sunday, and we will not put money into the offering plate again until we receive the next month's money. If we get paid every other week or twice a month, there will be at least two Sundays when we give something and two Sundays when we don't. If we freelance or are self-employed, what we give will change constantly.

That's the first way that proportional giving off the top changes the experience into something different from paying a bill. The amount of the cable bill is determined by how much we have agreed to pay regardless of what we have earned, but the amount of a proportional gift is determined solely by what God has given us.

There is one more important difference between proportional giving off the top and paying a bill. We make the proportional gift first, before we have even thought about the obligations we must meet. I pay bills twice a month, a schedule determined partly by how the various billing cycles fall and partly by when I get paid. The first thing I do is to review what money has come in since the last time I sat down to deal with money. My partner's pensions come once a month. I get paid every other week. Maybe there's money from the sale of one of his icons or my consulting. In order to calculate the tithe, I need to see what has come in. That means my first act is to see how God has provided for us.

Before I began tithing as an adult, I always started with how much I owed and then looked to see if there would be enough to cover the obligations. Beginning with what you have received is a different way of viewing the situation. The percentage gift then naturally becomes a thank offering for what God has given us, and it is also a real act of putting my trust in God's care, because I'm making that gift trusting that everything else will work out with God's help.

Here's how most people deal with their money.

1. See what your total obligations are, including your church pledge.

2. See if you have enough to cover your obligations.

Here's the experience of proportional giving off the top:

1. See how much God has given you since the last time you dealt with your money.

2. Give back to God the percentage you've decided on.

3. Turn to your obligations knowing and feeling that God is with you.

Money is a tool, and it is always working on us. If we use our money in the first way above, as most people do, money will be a tool that increases our anxiety. If we give proportionally off the top, money will be a tool that reinforces our trust in God's providence and care. If you are in a back-from-the-brink situation, you do not need any more anxiety, but you do need a deep assurance that you can "cast all your anxiety on him, because he cares for you" (1 Peter 5:7), and I dare to say that such an assurance can come *only* if you trust God with your money in the way that giving proportionally off the top causes you to trust.

The changes that happen in you when you actually put your financial life in God's hands by beginning to tithe are real, and those changes cannot be faked. You will actually experience that everything is a gift—not just money, but the things that happen to you and the people you meet. Your trust in God's care will grow because you are giving away more than you can rationally afford. And though you are giving more, because you are trusting in God's care, your anxiety about money will be lessened. Your conception of means and ends will be turned upside-down. Regardless of what we say, we normally act as if money is the end, and people are the means to that end. If I can convince someone to buy what I'm selling, I'll get the money. If we could just get twenty more people to join the parish and pledge, we could balance the budget. Proportional giving leads you to see people as ends in themselves, not as means to your end.

Proportional giving makes you understand in your bones that money is not a zero-sum game. Here's what I mean. I met recently with the stewardship committee of a parish that had come up with good words about everything being a gift from God to which we make a free and willing response. But the centerpiece of their pitch was a pie chart that had wedges of different sizes to represent housing, food, clothing, entertainment, and other expenses. There was a small wedge representing contributions to the church, and the slogan was, "Please increase the church wedge." Obviously no one involved in that graphic was giving proportionally off the top, because that's not how proportional givers think about money. Proportional givers do not feel that they have given something up because they are tithing. They do not have to sacrifice something in order to be generous. Another appeal that no tither would make is to ask people to give up their Starbucks one day a week so they can increase their pledge. That's all right, perhaps, as a discipline during Lent for a specific project, but it's a terrible way to talk about giving because it's a classic way of treating money as a zero-sum game: if I give you more, then I have less.

Tithing teaches us that money is elastic, not rigid. Money for tithers works like the manna in the wilderness—"those who gathered much have nothing over, and those who gathered little had no shortage" (Exodus 16:18). There will be enough to meet your needs. God will take care of you. If you are not tithing and your dollar gifts are far less than ten percent, you may not be able to make the switch all at once. That's all right. Change your pattern from so many dollars a week to some percentage *off the top,* and see how it goes. If it makes you anxious, lower the percentage until you feel liberated. Then see about ratcheting the percentage up bit by bit. That's how my mother did it as she got back to tithing after the upsets caused by the premature death of my father.

Tithing turns the money you have worked for into a gift, because you realize that the skills and talents you used to make the money are also gifts from God. We bring nothing to this endeavor; it's all a gift. And that means everything and everybody is a gift. You will interpret reality this way only if you have experienced in your financial life how dependent you are on God, and how trustworthy God is to those who depend on him.

All of these insights and experiences are necessary to effective turn-around work. The approach to your work that tithing helps instill has to do with seeing the parish you are rebuilding as a gift from God who wants it to thrive. God will give you the leads and possibilities and people you need in order to make it work. You will have very difficult work in developing those possibilities into reality, but God is also giving you the vision and stamina you need for the job. I have come to believe that church leaders cannot think and act out of that approach unless they have allowed God to transform their attitude about their own money. And, as I say, that transformation cannot be faked.

FIGURE OUT HOW TO DEAL WITH BEING TAKEN ADVANTAGE OF

There's a simple catch-22 in most turnaround situations. Effective leadership is essential in bringing a congregation back from the brink. When a congregation is at the brink, there will almost certainly not be enough money to pay for effective leadership. Therefore, this work, important as it is for the future of the church and as demanding as it is on you, will likely be compensated less adequately and more precariously than many other positions.

Under my partner's predecessor the parish had come close to closing. Partly because there was no money and partly because the vestry had no way of getting rid of the rector with whom they were very dissatisfied, they cut his salary year by year. By the time of his departure they were paying well below the diocesan minimum. The vestry called John at something close to the previous rector's final salary. John worked the first seven years of his twelve-year tenure at less than the diocesan minimum compensation. By that time the results of John's work were undeniable and the parish culture had gotten over its need to underpay the cleric. In other words, John had to work his way to the starting line, and we needed to figure out how to prevent the manifest unfairness of the situation from embittering us. You may be in a similar situation.

We need to think about this for a minute because resentment is the normal, unavoidable result of being in an objectively unfair situation. You are not wrong to feel angry and resentful. Rather, you need to figure out how to manage your normal and justified feelings of anger and resentment at being treated unfairly.

If the parish is able, with whatever level of difficulty, to pay for a full-time package at least at the diocesan minimum rate, that's great. You are not yet at the edge, though you may get there in a few years if the parish is balancing the budget by overdrawing the endowment. If you are really at the brink, however, you are probably there in some rather cobbled-together way. Maybe there's no outside assistance, so you are being paid "supply-plus" for half-time work, or they can come up with a half-time salary, but you have medical insurance through your spouse's job. In many such places the people and the vestry will want to pay you appropriately because they will be grateful for and excited by what you are doing, and they will try to get the compensation level up as fast as they can. Often, however, in addition to a tenuous financial situation, you will be dealing with some parishioners with control issues. They will resist the introduction of any health into the system because their power comes from the dysfunction. One of the ways such parishioners might try to sabotage you is by trying to keep your compensation not only lower than it should be, but also less than the parish can afford.

Maybe there is outside assistance from the judicatory or some other church entity. Yet those grants, wonderful as they are, may bring their own headaches, since perhaps they are not quite large enough, or the term of the grant may not be long enough, and the reporting requirements may be difficult. The decisions such funders make will, I hope, take the merits and needs of your situation in account, but there will always be competing considerations and too few resources to meet all the needs. You may be left short.

And while you are working hard to keep your parish from falling into the abyss, you will see well-paid colleagues who are leading their parishes placidly or headlong into ruin with no one at the parish or diocesan levels taking steps to correct or save the situation. A friend is right now having the unhappy experience of watching his successor at his former parish deplete the endowment my friend worked so hard to raise and to protect. They need to overspend the endowment now because the incumbent, with the bishop's support, is being paid more than twice the fair compensation my friend received, and the incumbent's poor leadership is causing people to leave in droves. Another friend's years of work building a college chaplaincy program were ruined before midterm exams of the semester following his departure. Competent, hardworking people are not just pained by such situations, they are angered by them, and their anger is justified.

Some things that may help create a defensive shield against the kind of resentment that will naturally occur in you as a result of being in an unfair and sometimes absurd situation are these:

- your wholehearted commitment to this particular kind of ministry;

- your satisfaction at seeing progress in a situation that seemed hopeless;

- the gratitude and devotion of the people in the congregation who see what you are doing and understand the financial and psychological costs.

These may help most of the time, but they do not erase the feelings. You will have a baseline level of resentment. The feelings can be managed so they do not render you ineffective, but they cannot be eliminated.

PUT ON THE WHOLE ARMOR OF GOD

All of the matters this chapter has treated are important parts of what you need to bring with you into a back-from-the-brink situation:

- ❧ a commitment to hold yourself strictly accountable to those you lead;

- ❧ the belief that something can be done in the situation you are entering;

- ❧ an intention to fall in love with the parish;

- ❧ respect for the laity and the conviction that they are the key to the solution, not part of the problem;

- ❧ a spiritual practice integrated with your work;

- ❧ the practice of proportional giving off the top;

- ❧ an awareness that resentment is a normal and justified response to any unfairness in your situation and an intention to stay alert to, and to manage, the negative effects that begin to appear.

There are different ways of describing this work. Although the heading of this section referenced Ephesians, I generally avoid the language of spiritual warfare, because in a war *people* are your enemies. In this work if you think you have enemies, you will undoubtedly begin to consider the people who oppose or resist you as your enemies. This will undermine or destroy your effectiveness because human opponents are not your enemies. However, there is definitely a spiritual conflict involved. I use the word "system" where St. Paul's said "powers and principalities." It is a struggle. It's hard work. There will be times when you do not see how to go forward. There will be other times when it feels as though the way forward is completely blocked. Those who are not good leaders themselves, perhaps including your bishop, will not understand what this work entails and may not be particularly supportive or grateful. If you lack any of the protections this chapter has discussed, you may be wounded in ways that will leave you unequal to the task. Bringing a parish back from the brink needs to be its own reward, because it is not, among other things, the best way to build your pension base.

CHAPTER FIVE

Getting Started

A thousand small adjustments turn rules into skills,
and then three smaller ones turn real skills into art.
— ADAM GOPNIK[22]

When you begin to work with a congregation that needs to be brought back from the brink, you will encounter things that once had life but have now become moribund. There will probably be serious building problems, a lack of money that cripples any level of healthy activity, and a dwindling and probably fractious group of faithful people who usually want to preserve and resuscitate the past while knowing that that is not possible. The things that are dead and dying will demand most of your time, energy, and mental space, and unless you can also see the possibilities for new life, those dead things will consume you.

Okay. Money trouble, building problems, toxic interpersonal relationships. Where do you start? You are somewhat like an EMT arriving at the scene of a multi-car accident. You are equipped and fortified with those interior dispositions and practices discussed in the previous chapter. Now you are faced with a messy situation. What do you do first? There is no program that you can simply begin to execute, but there are practices and approaches that can be used in a variety of circumstances.

GET THE GESTALT

You arrive with the conviction that the congregation has possibilities for a healthy future, and you have some idea of various ways to explore those possibilities. You are praying hard. You are reading everything you can about the congregation's history. You are listening to the aspirations and fears of the members. You are mulling the possibilities in your head all the time. You are identifying yourself with the place. You are coming to love the parish. Out of that emerges, not a detailed strategic plan, but a kind of insight and intuition about the totality of the parish.

You need to gain a deep identification and understanding of the essence of the entirety of the congregation—its past glories and defeats, its present reality, and its future possibilities. It is not enough to know what has worked in other places or to sense what is ultimately or theoretically possible; you need a feel for what is possible at this time and in this place. The possibilities that can come to birth will need to be genetically related to what has gone before. Remember, it's about the parish; it's not about you. You are not creating something here; you are bringing to birth the possibilities for the future that are inherent in the situation.

A turnaround situation requires change, and change is, of course, even more difficult in a failing congregation than in a thriving one. People in a failing situation are almost desperately attached to the familiar. When every aspect of a situation creates anxiety, and the future of the parish is in doubt,

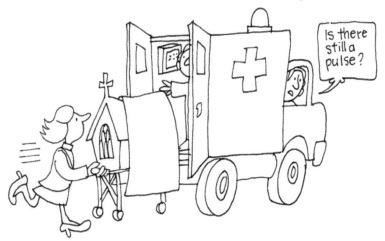

people find a sense of security in the familiar. And since failure is part of what is familiar, the introduction of healthy elements into the system will be resisted.

Getting the gestalt of this particular situation will help you avoid something that could wreck your efforts: trying to introduce something that may have worked elsewhere and might even work here someday, but will not work here at this time. A rector, newly arrived in a parish he knew was historically and self-consciously low-church, introduced Sanctus bells his second week and hung Stations of the Cross soon after. These were battles that never needed to be joined. These heedless and high-handed actions set the tone. His tenure was brief and stormy; he was finally forced out.

Gifted and hardworking leaders have come to grief over this. There was nothing wrong in the abstract with what they tried to do, but doing it right here and right now was a misjudgment that doomed their effectiveness. We need to be able to tell the difference between normal and inevitable resistance to health and the kind of reaction that warns us that we are trying to do something that is not congruent with the basic identity of the congregation. That identity is malleable, but only slowly. You will be able to float some things in your third year that would have sunk you in your first. Some things can be rushed, and others cannot. It is part of our job to know the difference. Developing deep identification with the nature of the place will help.

THE TOTALITARIAN VESTRY

When you walk into a situation that has had bad leadership, you are likely to find that the vestry wants to make every decision about everything in the parish. The worse the leadership has been, the more tightly they will cling to this practice. The urge is understandable. Maybe there was an overbearing priest who made financial decisions without seeking the vestry's approval. Whether or not there has been a settled priest, there will have been fights, mistrust, cliques, secrecy, people undermining others' efforts, and every kind of bad practice. And all this will have gone on as Sunday attendance fell, income dropped, and the buildings deteriorated.

The irresistible impulse in such chaotic situations is to concentrate all the power in the hands of the fewest possible people. Once that happens there will inevitably be a split between the vestry and the rest of the congregation. The latter will complain that the vestry is secretive and does not share information. The vestry will try to quash dissent through tighter controls. After one particularly awful vestry meeting, I realized that the dynamic around the table as the vestry had discussed members of the congregation had been what I imagine it is like when prison guards talk about how to deal with unruly inmates.

The only way you can deal with this dynamic is to build trust. A workshop or two that tries to delineate roles and responsibilities will not be sufficient. For quite some time you will want to bring to the vestry items that are canonically entirely under your control. Liturgical changes, your plans to revive the Sunday school, the Lenten program—in a normal parish you would simply report these to the vestry. In a turnaround situation you will want to give the vestry an opportunity to discuss, and, if trust is totally lacking, even formally approve, such matters. Remember, bad leadership brought the parish to the brink of failure. You are the new leader. Why shouldn't you be distrusted? It is necessary to earn the trust of the people you are serving. If you show yourself genuinely devoted only to the health of the parish and not to your own status or position, you will earn that trust, and the vestry will begin to be able to concern itself with its proper governance functions and leave the management of the program to you. But this cannot be rushed, and it will be very difficult to put up with.

BE TRANSPARENT

We all know that no matter how assiduously we communicate, some people will always say they do not know what is going on. Most congregations near death do a bad job of communicating, and people are often right to say they don't know what is happening. Parishes in survival mode concentrate power in the hands of a few. In situations where there has been bad leadership, information is power, so the few with power will not willingly share much information. The vestry will probably not receive useful financial reports regularly or at all. The accounting system will probably be poorly organized, so producing such reports will be time-consuming, if not impossible. Those with the power will probably think that if they have managed to keep it going from one meeting to the next, it should be enough to tell the vestry that. In one parish, there was never a revenue and expense statement, and the chair of the finance committee's report always was that the bills had been paid and that there was no money. Both assertions were always partially, and sometimes wholly, untrue, but there was no way to challenge either the information or her belligerent mien, so the report always served to forestall questions and keep her firmly in control.

And control is generally the besetting problem in failing parishes. When some people say they have not been informed, they mean that they were not part of making the decision. When you suggest an idea for the first time, there will be those who will be angry that they were not consulted before you spoke for the first time about it. Because there has probably been bad leadership or no leadership before you, the vestry will likely want to control every little thing about the management of the operation, to the detriment of their governance responsibilities. They will want to decide things that are canonically the responsibility of the clergy, such as the content of the services and the use of the parish buildings for parish functions. Key leaders will see just about everything you do as a threat to their control—and they are right.

There will also be deep reservoirs of suspicion and distrust; through repeated hearings you will become able to recite the litanies of the past wrongs the people did to one another. It takes about three years of good leadership for people to stop talking constantly about the bad old days. You just have to wait it out while doing everything to make it better. Your job is, I think, to listen with sympathy and good humor, to take it in so you get the lay of the land, and not to engage much with that history. It is sometimes difficult not to take sides in some of these feuds, because people will have done some really bad things to others, but from what I have seen, it is almost always a mistake to do so.

The main thing is to set a different tone going forward. Be honest, accountable, and kind. Freely admit mistakes and apologize for errors, especially to the difficult people who are looking for something to complain about. You are trying to make yourself as approachable as possible so people can tell you what they think; constant, sincere apologies for little things help a lot in this regard. Model accountability in public and in private, and then you can begin suggesting privately how the person you are talking to can be more accountable in her actions.

This is easier said than done. It took most of yesterday, for example, and several drafts of e-mails before I had worked through my feelings about the following situation. The gas company was unable for a long time to gain access to read the meters. The treasurer had kept information about the meter reading dates from the sexton as part of her campaign against him. When the company finally added a penalty for failing to provide access, she threw that bomb at the end of a vestry meeting, blaming the sexton and telling me—five weeks on the job—that I was not supervising him correctly. I informed the officers the next day that the sexton had dealt with the situation, and the charge would be removed from the bill. I added, "Going forward, I will be happy to take responsibility to make sure things like this happen when needed. It would be helpful to hear about such matters as soon as possible—no need to surprise me at a vestry meeting!" The treasurer was understandably irate—but quite out of proportion to my offense. By the end of the next day I was able to say, "I apologize to you all. I should not have made the dig in my first e-mail about being surprised at the vestry meeting with the National Grid matter. However, if anyone besides the treasurer knew about the matter before the meeting started, then I should have been included in that group. If more than one person knew before the meeting started, then I was right to feel surprised and blindsided. No one had told me previously that there was any history of a problem with National Grid gaining access to the meters. Nevertheless, even if I was right to feel blindsided, I was not right to make that dig, and I apologize."

Some clergy, especially women, have said they can be reluctant to apologize, because parishioners of both genders are still likely to take a woman less seriously as a leader than a man. Apologies may seem like self-abasement, but they do not have to be. I believe that the apology I made to the officers of the vestry is an example of one that takes responsibility while still maintaining one's dignity in a firm but civil way. No one will always handle difficult relationships faultlessly. I am convinced that the more difficult the relationship, the more vital it is for us to apologize for errors of tone or judgment, without groveling or pretending to be sorry for things for which we should not be apologetic. All of us probably need to hone our apology skills so that we can name our mistakes without losing standing in the eyes of others. An unwillingness to apologize when necessary in an appropriate way will cause others to lose more respect for us because we will appear defensive, and defensiveness is always a sign of weakness.

At one parish the former rector had set people against one another so they would not turn on him. There were angry outbursts at the coffee hour, malevolent glances, and a habit of complaining. In my first sermon I said I intended to be forthright, honest, and kind, and I asked people to call me to account if I was not acting in accordance with these intentions. And I asked people to be forthright, honest, and kind with me. A few weeks later I began to ask people to be as kind to one another as they were to me. I observed that we are not only kind to the people we like, but we tend to like the people we are kind to.

I kept trying to model kindness in all my interactions and to urge kindness in sermon after sermon and in group and individual conversations. I began using a form of blessing every week that contained the exhortation to "be kindly affectioned one to another." It seemed like trying to cut granite with a rubber knife. Then one day an experienced complainer said, "I know you want us to be kind, but I just can't be kind to *her*." Some months later she handled with adroit good humor a conversation with a fellow parishioner that once would have become ugly. Then she looked over to where I was sitting and said, "Did you see what I did?" I gave her a big hug.

Over time there was an appreciable change in the atmosphere and spirit of the congregation. Not everyone got the point, but enough did to make a real difference. I would have been wholly ineffective if people had not seen that I was making a real effort to practice what I was preaching—and apologizing when I failed.

Perhaps interpersonal conflict is not as rife in your congregation as in that one, but you will almost certainly find some aspect of parish life where you can do your best to model a certain kind of behavior and encourage others to emulate it.

REMEMBER: YOU ARE INDISPENSABLE, BUT IT'S NOT ABOUT YOU

Here, not for the last time, we encounter the paradoxical reality that, while an effective leader is indispensable in making a congregation thrive, the life of the congregation belongs to the congregation, not to the leader. I have made clear how vital I think leadership is, but not just any kind of leadership, certainly not the kind of leadership that tries to make the parish into what the leader wants.

Books of an evangelical orientation on revitalizing churches hold up a kind of leadership that makes me deeply uncomfortable. "You are the primary shaper of your church's values, beliefs, strategy, and direction,"[23] pastors are told. Another book suggests that the worship services be "imprinted with the style, attitude and character of the new pastor."[24]

We would be more likely to say that the Prayer Book, the Bible, and the hymnal shape our beliefs, and many of us find it distracting when a priest imprints the liturgy with her personal style—or at least we find it distracting when *other* clergy do that! On Good Friday in one parish without a regular priest, the supply priest entered the church in silence, then threw himself prone for several minutes in the center aisle of a church with high box pews. All that could be heard was the thump of his hand beating his breast. Since people could not see him, no one knew what had happened. Instead of moving people to meditate on the Passion, that performance was simply a distraction from the solemn rite.

We do, I hope, subordinate our personal preferences and to some extent our personalities to the rite we are performing. We follow the rubrics even if we might have written some differently. We follow the parish customs even if we would rather do it some other way. This is good for us. Doing the liturgy in ways we might not prefer provides us all—especially bishops, priests, and deacons—with physical, tangible reminders that we are part of a body of which we are not the head.

On the other hand, we do not become automatons. Clergy are not interchangeable widgets. We cannot coast and depend on our formularies and customaries to do all the work for us. The words of the liturgy and the manner of its performance make up only part of the story. The manner of our leadership is experienced in the ineffable but unmistakable spirit we convey in the liturgy and in the rest of our ministry. Are we fully engaged or phoning it in? Are we communicating something of the love of God or our need to be loved? Are we speaking God's word, or are we trying to get people to do things that would make our jobs easier? Are we giving an authentic witness or making people uncomfortable by our self-importance or unbelief?

This is related to St. Paul's habit of urging the churches to which he is writing to be imitators of him. The admonitions of my Midwestern boyhood make me loath at least to seem to call attention to myself in that way. I thought about casting the story of preaching kindness in the preceding section in the third person as if it had happened to someone else, but that would have evaded what is precisely the issue. The "product" of the faith is transformed lives. God can use lives that are being transformed into the divine likeness to build a just and peaceable kingdom. The point for us is not finishing the kingdom; that will come in God's own time. The point for us is to become the kind of people who *want* God's will to be done in our lives as it is in heaven and who become different as a result.

St. Paul does not say we should imitate him, period. He says, "Be imitators of me, as I am of Christ" (1 Corinthians 11:1). We want people to imitate us only in the ways that we imitate Christ. The point is to live as Christ lives, but we need visible human examples of that kind of living. Such examples are certainly provided by many of the faithful, but we leaders also need to provide those examples to the best of our abilities.

If we do not at least long to live our lives differently from how we would have lived them without being joined to the body of Christ in baptism, then we are indeed just clanging cymbals. Christian leadership is not about charisma, personality, or ambition; rather, it is about wanting to lead lives worthy of emulation. And that includes appropriate acknowledgments of our failures to live such lives.

GET THE RIGHT PEOPLE
ON BOARD

You cannot do this alone. And even if you could do it alone, it would be a bad idea. From the first day you are trying to build something that will outlast you. You need staff, volunteer or paid, to build that with you, and they need to be the right individuals. When you arrive at your turnaround situation, you may well find that you do not have the staff you need and that the staff you have are not the right people. It will not be a single day's work to address such a situation.

You may be thinking that you wish you had any staff at all when you started. Let me clarify. My discussion of staffing assumes a physical plant that needs work, but that could also provide resources for the budget. The three turnaround situations in which I have been involved have been parishes with small attendance but substantial plants. In each case, figuring out how to derive income from the plant has been an essential part of the turnaround. Having the maintenance staff necessary to put the buildings in rentable shape, to keep them in shape, and to provide landlord services to the renters is necessary in order to realize the income the parish needs.

I know of two priests leading successful turnarounds in plants that are very small. When average Sunday attendance neared fifty in one of those places, a second service had to be added because the church is so tiny. In those situations the pledge and plate from an attendance of fifty to seventy

people can support a half-time priest and the building, and no paid staff apart from a musician and a cleaner may be necessary.

I have fewer ideas, however, about how to turn around parishes with low attendance and substantial or historic plants that have no possibility of rental income. One parish I know has a 140-year-old complex with a church that seats 250 but no parish hall or other space that could be used by others. The congregation of about thirty can afford only a supply priest. The historic church and rectory are beautiful, though in need of major work. Because the demographics of the area are good, it might be possible to build a congregation of 125 to 150 that could support a full-time priest and the building on pledge and plate alone, but that could happen only if outside resources were available to pay a turnaround priest for at least several years. I do not see that in the cards, so this may be one of those situations that ultimately may not be able to be saved.

The closer the problem staff position is to the center of power and control in the failing system, the more difficult it will be to address. Make the progress you can make where you can make it. Even if you identify immediately that the secretary is a big problem, you may be well advised to wait before doing something about it; she may be tied to the person who controls the money. You may not be able to do anything about her until other things in the system have become healthier. The organist too usually has a constituency.

If there is a way to address the sexton's situation, that is often a good place to start. The right sexton will be an important factor in getting people to feel better about the buildings, and that helps the parish system take a big step forward toward health. If some of the rentals are private parties, you need the right sexton to staff the parties, recommend others who can work the parties, and perhaps do some of the marketing and bookings. Do not hire by job description or by resume. Of course you need to be clear about what the duties are, but you are looking for the right person who can assist you in moving the whole operation in the direction it needs to go. You may not be able to pay adequately, but if you can offer the possibility of extra earnings from the rentals, that can help you get the kind of enterprising person you need.

You need to think ahead when filling positions, just as you do when leasing a copier. You do not lease a new copier that can do only what you're already doing. You want a machine that can allow you to do all kinds of things you can't do now. You want staff that will take the job beyond the current duties. You want them to catch and share the vision you have for the things that can be created. Even if you are sorry to see the incumbent retire or resign, every opportunity to hire is a precious gift in any situation, but particularly in a turnaround. Prepare for these opportunities, and make the most of them when they occur.

ADDRESS THE MAJOR SOURCES OF ANXIETY

The first order of business is to identify the major sources of anxiety in the congregation and to begin to address them in visible, tangible ways. The sources of anxiety will probably be easy to figure out: the closer you are to the abyss, the more it will almost certainly be the state of the buildings and the lack of money that are making people anxious and quarrelsome. It is necessary to find ways to make people see that the parish is making progress with those issues. It is no good to say that you will concentrate on growth or program and somehow that will fix the budget deficit and the building problems. Unless the plant is very small, it won't work that way.

My second or third week at Intercession, a young visitor asked me as I was greeting him after the service, "What volunteer opportunities are there here?" I almost blurted out, "All we do here is pay Con Ed." Because there was a monthly crisis about getting the utility bill paid, people could not think about anything else, and the urgency occupied a lot of my mental space as well. I knew we had to get the operating budget stabilized so that people could turn their thoughts to what could happen in those buildings. Then we could tell future visitors that we were doing more than keeping the lights on.

The buildings and the budget are so important that each requires its own chapter in this book. Even if your congregation is not at the brink of collapse, your budget may have weaknesses that need attention. The congregation may be too reliant on sources of income other than plate and pledge. For example, if you have an endowment, you may well be overspending it to support the operating budget. This is an unsustainable trend that needs to be turned around. The buildings may not be in terrible shape, but accomplishing something significant and positive with the buildings will be an enormous shot in the arm to the parish's confidence. Every priest I have spoken to who is doing this work has said that completing a building project or a capital campaign was a turning point for the congregation.

You will not be able to distract people from the things that are making them anxious. The only way around anxiety is through it. To gain credibility and trust—and to help bring the congregation back from the dead—you have to identify and start addressing the major sources of anxiety.

DON'T SWEAT THE
SMALL STUFF

In a congregation that is near the brink your role is much closer to that of an orthopedic surgeon in a trauma unit than that of a plastic surgeon. The desirable is not necessarily the vital. I encourage you to think very carefully about everything you decide to devote your energy to. Keep a sense of proportion. Some things are more important than others. If the ship is taking on water, you really want to focus everyone's attention on bailing and fixing the hole. At first, leave the deck chairs where they are even if you hate their configuration. Here's why.

Suspicion is a powerful corrosive. Trust is the lubrication that permits a system to move. There will be no trust in a system that is at the brink of failure. Previous leaders will have acted in ways that destroyed trust and optimism. That's why the system will be locked, and everyone's motives will be suspect.

It requires time and patient work to build up enough trust so that things can start to move. While you are building up these reservoirs of trust, make changes only where absolutely necessary. At this point every change will cost you a significant chunk of people's goodwill. Even if it is a matter over which the canons give you total control, making a change will come at a cost. You need to do a careful analysis of the costs and the benefits of the change.

If you want to make a possibly controversial change in some relatively small matter, examine yourself. Why are you doing this? Why can't you live with it as it is? Is it just your preference? Because it is an area under your canonical control, do you think you should be able to have it the way you want? Do you think that, having made the request, it would be a sign of weakness to back down, so you must now insist?

Sometimes a small thing isn't so small, and there is a strategic reason to make a change at once. A friend in a turnaround situation found that the parishioners each had their own coffee mugs for the coffee hour. The mugs were laid out on the counter. A visitor reached for a mug, not knowing the protocol. A rather bossy hospitality chair took the mug from her hand saying, "That's not for you," and handed her a styrofoam cup. The visitor was embarrassed, and my friend was incensed. Fortunately he did not speak to the hospitality chair until he had calmed down. He then worked out with her that the parish would buy some mugs that said, "We're glad you're here" and put them on the counter. Old-timers, if they like, can go into the kitchen to take their personal mugs from the wall where they hang.

No one is made to feel awkward, and no one gets an environmentally un-
friendly cup.

When you are thinking of changing a small thing in the parish, consider
asking yourself these questions first.

- § Will doing this change make a difference in bringing the parish
  back from the brink?

- § Will it make enough of a difference so that the contention the
  change might cause will be a reasonable price to pay?

If the answer to either question is no, then it may be wiser to hold back
and save your energy and political capital for the things that matter. If the
answer to both questions is yes, then you still need to figure out how to
do it in the way that will cause the least friction possible. My friend could
have caused a major firestorm over the coffee mugs by handling the matter
less adroitly.

Once you have demonstrated again and again that your motives are not
self-interested, making changes becomes easier. At the beginning, however,
don't spend your capital on things that can easily wait.

START TALKING,
START DOING

From the time you arrive, start talking about the ideas you have that will begin to move the congregation in a healthy direction. Communicating the fundamental idea that you believe there is a future for the congregation is perhaps more important than your ideas about what that future could be like. Those ideas will be subject to modification, but your belief in the future is like yeast that begins to leaven a sodden lump. Since parishes are seldom brought to the brink of failure by effective leaders, it will probably have been some time since the people have heard from a leader who sincerely believes that this parish can be turned around.

They will want to believe you, and they will also resist, since they have probably been deceived before. Their resistance will be frustrating, but it will be good to try to avoid the mistake many people make of dismissing the past and moving on too quickly. It is easy, particularly if you have fully formed ideas about what can be done, to think impatiently, "Well, I'm here now. What is past doesn't matter." William Faulkner wisely observed, "The past is never dead. It's not even past." As important as your contribution may be in the history of the parish, your tenure is only one moment in that history, not the culmination of it.

In one small city in 1969 the diocesan office forced three parishes to merge. Instead of choosing a new dedication for the new entity, the members insisted that the merged parish be called by the three saints' names of the constituent congregations; this decision did not bode well. In the late 1990s, just before a vestry meeting, I asked the treasurer if she could get a copy of the previous year's parochial report. A former member of one of the three parishes, whose building had burned, she replied, "Oh, I'm from St. Peter's; I don't know where these St. Swithin's people keep anything." The merger had taken place nearly thirty years before, but it might as well have happened that morning. In all those years the leadership had never been able to offer a shared vision for the future that could enlist the people's support, so they had stayed mired in the past. And that is not surprising, because there had been no forward-looking vision offered when the merger was done. There were three dwindling congregations and a lack of money to keep up three plants, so why not consolidate into one? It appeared a sensible move, but because it was all about acquiescing to decline, further decline was the unsurprising result. The combined congregation in a small plant has been receiving diocesan assistance ever since the merger.

Stick tight to the belief that a healthy future is possible, and hang very loose to the ideas you have about getting there. Some of your ideas will work; some of them will fail. Some will need to be changed; others will need to wait a while. Talk to everyone you meet inside and outside the congregation about their ideas. Listen carefully. Don't dismiss even things that sound foolish. I will go so far as to say that if you do not begin to see possibilities and opportunities that you had not thought of, it may mean that you are too focused to your own ideas to listen and watch for what God is putting in your path.

IF MANNA FALLS FROM HEAVEN, EAT IT

A friend doing a very successful turnaround in a small suburban community told me that she finds herself constantly preaching about manna. The Bible makes it clear that manna is something unexpected, something "with which neither you nor your ancestors were acquainted." It is both a sign

of God's faithful provision for a people wandering in the wilderness and an educational tool to help them understand "that one does not live by bread alone, but by every word that comes from the mouth of the LORD" (Deut. 8:3).

You will remember that first, the people were suspicious of the manna when it first appeared and second, they grew tired of it. The point is that we do not always recognize or approve of what God provides. Maybe we have our own ideas about what constitute theologically correct sources of revenue for a parish. I encourage you to get rid of all your preconceived notions in this regard. If you are in a turnaround situation, do not spurn on principle any possibilities that present themselves. That's like longing for the leeks and garlic of Egypt and refusing to eat the manna God has sent you from heaven. You may think film shoots are disrespectful and private parties indecorous. God may disagree with you. If it might be manna, say thank you to the God who sent it your way, then pick it up and eat it.

You will need to work on many fronts at the same time—building problems, paying bills, interpersonal relationships, pastoral care, morale, staff oversight, education, fundraising, stewardship formation, setting up tables and chairs, and whatever else comes your way. All of it is important, and you need to start pushing forward wherever you see the opportunity. You need the eyes to see that the ideas and people that present themselves are manna. My advice is to try just about anything. Say a tentative "yes" to everything you can, and see how it works out. As soon as we got liability insurance, our first program at Intercession was to host a shelter for homeless LBGT youth. There was some hesitation, but in general people were so happy to have *something* going on that there was not a big blow-up, even when we had to stop the shelter because the supervision and security supplied by the program were inadequate. The vestry moved easily into trying another program. We all learned that there was no downside if we tried something that did not work. You just try something else, not forgetting, of course, the lessons you picked up from the last thing.

Consider every person you meet, every idea anybody has, and every proposal that comes your way a gift from a God who is trying to help you. Don't reject anything out of hand or on principle. God always chooses unexpected and even disreputable instruments to accomplish his purposes. We need to hone our ability to recognize manna. And we need to remember that manna was an acquired taste. Acquiring a taste for it and helping the people of the parish acquire a taste for it is a big part of the job.

PERSONAL GENEROSITY
PRIMES THE PUMP

At every parish on the brink that I have ever known the people who remain really want the parish to survive. However, because there has not been transparency about money and because there has not been any vision of the future articulated, people are holding back. They have put money into the parish, and they will put in more, but there simply cannot be a spirit of willing generosity in a place where there is no trust and no vision. Usually some have cut back on their giving because of the contention and suspicion.

That's where your money comes in. Part of your job is to model the kind of selfless personal generosity you hope the people will adopt. You cannot ask people to become generous with their money if you are not generous with yours. Make it clear right away that your tithe or proportional gift is going to the parish. If you are not tithing or practicing proportional giving off the top at some level, please think about adopting the practice. It changes you; it changes your relationship to your money; it changes how you think about money in general. As I have said, these changes are real, and they cannot be faked. And, at least in my experience, a transformed relationship with money is essential in order to be able to do a turnaround.

You are probably walking into a log jam where everything is impossible because there is too little money and it is being controlled inappropriately. People are upset that the buildings are dirty, but the treasurer cannot or will not buy cleaning supplies for the sexton to use. Maybe the parish provides housing for the sexton to justify the low hourly wage, but the apartment is hardly habitable, and still the vestry members mutter about him using utilities for free. You need to get something moving; spending your money is the best way to do it. This is also why you need to be in love with the place from before Day One. That love helps move you to want to spend your own money without resentment.

At the end of my first week at St. Mary's in Brooklyn I e-mailed one of the sextons at Intercession, "Just wanted you to know I took the sexton at St. Mary's to Home Depot today to buy him materials, tools, and supplies so he can do his job. Thank God there's already a good sexton here, competent, friendly, and willing, but he's underpaid and the apartment he has is a wreck and some on the vestry want him to pay rent. Does it all sound familiar?" Of course it did, since every aspect of the situation had been the same at Intercession.

Early in his tenure in a turnaround situation in the early 1980s, my partner proposed a Lenten series that would consist of Evensong, a light supper, and a program. The anxious—and controlling—objections were, "Well, who will come? What if nobody comes?" We'll invite everyone, we said, and we'll be happy with whoever shows up. "Who will play the organ? We can't pay the organist for another service." No problem, I said, I can play the organ. "What about the supper? Who will pay for the food?" We'll take care of it for all five weeks, John said. As I recall, about eighteen people came the first week, and the program went fine. One devoted woman said, "This supper doesn't look hard to do. I'll bring it next week." Others chimed in, and within minutes the other four Sundays were taken care of. We were prepared to do all the suppers as a gift. People felt free to offer to help precisely because we did not ask them to. There was no obligation or pressure. It was a tiny demonstration of how what St. Paul calls "the matter of giving and receiving" (Philippians 4:15) can work, and it set a tone going forward. This past Lent exactly the same thing happened at the Wednesday night program we held at St. Mary's.

When you are visibly generous, people learn two important things. First, they learn that you are identifying completely with the situation. You are not holding yourself apart. It is as important to you as it is to them, and although you are new, you love the place as much as they do. Second, they learn that it is not dangerous or difficult to be generous. It is not good money after bad; rather, it is a way of moving into the future you've been talking about. And it doesn't cost that much. It is within the capacity of us all to be as generous as we want to be. It begins to break the log jam. People respond to generosity with generosity; the system starts to get healthier, and the cash crunch eases, allowing more to start happening.

Strategic use of your personal generosity is a way of jumpstarting what needs to get done. Maybe it would take several rancorous vestry meetings to try to get them to see that if they want the windows cleaned, they should not expect the sexton to buy the window cleaner himself. So you buy it for him, and the windows get cleaned. As people are feeling better about that, you can reinforce the lesson that good employees need to be supported, given what they need to do their work, and thanked daily for the good job they do.

Spending your own money is a way to break open a situation in which people are afraid or are exercising an inappropriate kind of control in the community. Offering to provide the suppers at the Lenten evening programs was a way of showing people that they did not need to be afraid. With respect to control issues, you will find that buying supplies for the sexton will frequently offend whoever controls the money. This will catch you off guard if you are not prepared for that response. You need to remember that communicating anxiety to others is a way of maintaining control in a group. In a failing situation the treasurer is understandably anxious, but she has usually also come to like the kind of control that communicating her anxiety gives her. So whoever controls the money, paradoxically, is likely to be the one who most strenuously resists doing anything that will improve the financial situation and will be the last one to acknowledge that things are improving.

It is very difficult to bear in mind that this dynamic is part of a failing system; it's not just a personal trait on the part of the treasurer. It will be especially difficult to remember this if, as is likely, the treasurer is undermining your efforts, second-guessing your decisions, and going behind your back. You may respond inappropriately sometimes because this stuff can really get under your skin, but try to remember that as the situation improves, most people will move toward a healthier place. They will have more confidence in the future; they will trust you because you have demonstrated yourself trustworthy; and they will want to seize the opportunities God sends the parish. Those who stay in the old ways of anxiety, distrust, and control will sideline themselves because people will have experienced how much better it is to be healthy. It takes several years, however, and it can drive you nuts in the meantime.

Money is a tool that can be put to many uses. You need to be sure that you use your personal funds purely in pursuit of the good of the parish and its staff, not in order to manipulate others or to get your own way. There is a fine line here, but if you bring to your work the self-awareness good leadership requires, you will be able to tell where the line is. There is a difference between buying the floor stripper and wax the sexton needs and, say, personally paying soloists so you will enjoy the music more or providing a lunch every week after the service rather than the simple coffee hour the parish wants. The first is meeting a basic need, and in my experience it causes people to move more quickly toward a situation in which the parish can pay for what it needs. When the other happens, people feel that you have done a kind of manipulative end-run around them, and they are right.

SUMMING UP

Much of what I have said so far may seem too passive, because I have counseled patience and a certain abnegation of self. Aren't we supposed to put forth our bold vision about what can happen, start making those things happen, and tell people to get to work or get out of the way? In my experience, that's not the way to bring about change with the members of a congregation on the brink of failure. Turnarounds may be more difficult than new starts in this regard. A new start may be comparable to the pre-Constantinian church, while a turnaround is like the post-Constantinian church. Turnarounds must deal with the debris of past failures as well as the dead weight of past glories. If there are possibilities in the situation, I think the best way to turn them into reality is to work them into the existing life of the congregation while working the existing life of the congregation into something that looks to the future with hope.

The method, I hope, is largely laid out. The method demands things like the following:

- ♪ a wide but very flexible vision;

- ♪ strict mutual accountability;

- ♪ generosity of spirit and of purse;

- ♪ patience;

- ♪ forbearance;

- ♪ a willingness to acknowledge shortcomings; and

- ♪ an ability to recognize the gifts God is trying to give you.

Most of the method is the interior work necessary to make you act like that kind of person. I will clarify that you do not have to *be* that kind of person—no one can be—but you must at least as often as you can *act as if* you are that kind of person.

We will now see examples of the method in dealing with the three most urgent concerns in a turnaround—buildings, budgets, and interpersonal relationships.

CHAPTER SIX

Get Control of the Buildings

*When Solomon had finished building the house of the LORD
and the king's house, and all that Solomon desired to build,
the LORD appeared to Solomon a second time, as he had appeared
at Gibeon. The LORD said to him, "I have heard your prayer and
your plea, which you made before me; I have consecrated this
house that you have built, and put my name there forever;
my eyes and my heart will be there for all time."*
— 1 KINGS 9:1–3

We might want spiritual concerns to be the drivers of the revitalization of a parish. However, in my observation and experience, if there is one key to the turnaround liturgy, that key is getting on top of the buildings.

If the physical plant is in terrible shape, it will be the major source of anxiety and shame for the people. You must do whatever is necessary to get control of the buildings so that people can begin to think about other things with hope for the future. Of course you have to work on more than one front, but if you do not address the major sources of anxiety from the very beginning, you will not make progress.

Even if the buildings are in good shape, every priest I have spoken to who has done this work has identified a major building project as a turning point in the congregation's comeback. In one parish a roof had been replaced, and that was a watershed moment. In another, getting the derelict rectory fixed up was that kind of turning point in the life of the congregation.

The importance buildings have in our lives is not surprising, because we are body-selves. The places where our bodies spend time have an effect on us. Whether large or small, grand or plain, the buildings in which we worship will both shape and express our feelings and our attitudes. The condition of the buildings affects us for good or ill. And the way the buildings look tells you how the congregation feels about itself.

At the same time, the buildings are not an end in themselves. We have buildings so that we can do the work God has given us to do. We do not keep up our buildings *instead of* fulfilling our mission; we take care of our buildings *so that* we can fulfill our mission. When the buildings are poorly kept, the people are aware that the parish's ability to fulfill its mission is impaired. Clergy who are well-intentioned but misguided often make things worse by buying into the false dichotomy between buildings and mission.

Let's make that act of translation again and consider the importance of the physical plant in non-church terms. Could a college operate without classrooms and dorms? Could a museum not have galleries and storage? What message is conveyed by dilapidated public schools, and art galleries with cracked ceilings or peeling paint on the walls? Why do we think it would be any different with church facilities? The  buildings are an expression of who we see ourselves to be. They do not need to be fancy, but whether large or small, elaborate or simple, old or new, they need to be clean, well-kept, safe, and welcoming. If the buildings convey the sense that the people love them and care for them, that will help newcomers love them as well.

GET RID OF THE JUNK

We have seen that many mainline churches today are obsessed with the maintenance of the institution, as they are either already in crisis or see a crisis looming not too far down the road. Congregations have aged and dwindled to the point where sometimes only 10 or 15 percent of the seating capacity of their beautiful historic buildings is used on Sundays, and they have depleted their endowments. One of the primary ways leaders have dealt with the loss of income caused by the erosion of membership and attendance is by deferring maintenance on buildings that are now unattractive, unusable, or even unsafe.

It is no longer possible for many parishes to pretend that things can go on this way much longer. Very likely the congregation is anxious because of the state of the physical plant. You would not send your child to a college that could not maintain its buildings and grounds; you would not think of checking into a hospital that was not fully accessible and air-conditioned. Despite our valiant attempts to whistle amid the falling plaster, we know that we are in fact ashamed to have outsiders see our beloved buildings in the state we have permitted them to attain.

The grounds, the buildings, and the contents of the buildings are physical expressions of the spirit of those who occupy them. In every case of which I am aware, as the congregation declines, the buildings deteriorate, the shrubbery gets overgrown, and stuff accumulates.

In one parish the entrances were almost hidden by bushes that had been allowed to get out of control. We organized a clean-up day and cut everything back. It did not solve all the problems; several yew bushes had been let go to the point that they finally had to be taken out. However, the impression made by the buildings was different because they finally appeared to be cared for. The clean-up lifted the spirits of the parishioners because it showed them that something could be done and led them to think of other things that could be done.

Almost every parish—and certainly every parish on the brink—could benefit from one or more dumpsters. Useless stuff just multiplies, reflecting and reinforcing the people's sense that the situation cannot be addressed. One summer the youth group from a parish outside New York City came to Intercession for a mission trip. They painted several spaces and did other jobs, but the most important contribution they made was to pay for two thirty-cubic-yard dumpsters. We cleaned out the choir room, which had been difficult to enter because of the junk that had piled up after the demise of the choir. All kinds of spaces throughout the complex were cleared out. It was finally possible to walk into a room and think of the possible uses to which it could be put instead of being demoralized by the clutter.

One of the places things will accumulate is in the vestibules of the church itself. At Intercession the outdoor Christmas crèche and the snowblower were stored in the north porch all spring and summer, so the narthex sometimes smelled of gasoline. In one parish the north vestibule had not been opened for years because it was full of stuff. There was a profusion of tables in the back of the church piled high with old tracts and out-of-date schedules and papers. Thus the very part of the buildings that any visitor will be certain to see assertively proclaims that the parish system is failing and has come to be comfortable with that. Most people will be happy to see things cleaned up, but you can expect some to be upset.

It was no accident that Intercession's dumpsters needed to be paid for by outsiders. Because our financial system had been producing failure, I had to come to terms with the fact that failure was what it had been designed to produce. Expect resistance to getting a dumpster; whoever controls the money will say that the parish cannot afford it, and it is not a priority. Such a reaction is the normal resistance of a dysfunctional system to the introduction of any healthy element. Cleaning things up will make people feel that failure is not inevitable, and that is a threat to a system designed to fail. In a failing parish, money is almost always under the control of people who have become more invested in their power and control than in the good of the parish. They are part of the system that resists health.

You may need to come up with another way to finance the dumpster, but get a dumpster, and trim the hedges as quickly as you can. Everybody will feel better.

A word about bathrooms
You can tell a lot about a parish by how free things are of overgrowth and clutter, but you can sometimes get an unsettling view into the soul of the parish by looking at the bathrooms. Rusty partitions, inoperable or missing

stall doors, mold on the walls, deteriorated floor tiles, unpleasant odors, leaky sinks with no hot water—the bathrooms show you how people really feel; they are reliable barometers of a parish's self-esteem.

Bathrooms are not cheap to renovate, and custodial services are often in short supply, but those considerations are no excuse for dreadful bathrooms. I have seen plenty of old bathrooms that are freshly painted and scrubbed clean, with perhaps some little decoration. On a visit to one parish I was positively heartened by a bathroom with ancient fixtures and wooden partition a century old, because of its thrifty cleanliness and a few little touches that showed that the people cared. Redo the bathrooms (and probably the kitchen) as soon as you can, but in the meantime they do not have to be disgusting. They can be clean and serviceable, and can thus let people know someone cares.

Parishes need to make sure the messages such spaces communicate about them are the messages they want others to receive.

TACKLE THE IMMEDIATE PROBLEM

There is likely to be one very serious building problem when you begin. At Intercession it was a quarter-million dollars of work on the heating system that had to be done before the next heating season. At St. Mary's the parish house had the kind of roof through which you could see the sky. There is not one way to approach these problems, but there are a few elements common to many such situations.

The first common theme is that people are likely to be paralyzed by the problem. This paralysis will probably express itself in this way: instead of concentrating on how to get the resources together that will fix the problem, they will instead squabble over who took what step and whether they were authorized to do that.

At St. Mary's so much water had penetrated for so long that about 500 square feet of the relatively new flooring looked more like the rolling waves of the sea than a surface on which were once placed tables and chairs. While people acknowledged the seriousness of the situation, their energy was not directed toward fixing it, but toward fighting about the process that had been used to solicit the bids. The real issue was that there was no money to pay the deposit to any contractor to get the job going. I said, "I will ask the diocese to loan us the money for the deposit so we can get started. Let's adopt a motion to accept a bid contingent on getting the loan and to agree to take on the loan contingent on the bishop's willingness to make it." The diocesan office cut the check within days, and the work began within two weeks.

The funding for the heating system work at Intercession was more intricate. It was a combination of a grant and loan from the diocese, a grant from another parish, and permission from the state to redirect for this purpose part of a "member-item" grant made to refurbish a community space.

You will notice that in neither case did any of the initial money for the immediate building crisis come from the congregation. When things are slipping into the abyss, people simply will not put more money into it. Some positive things have to happen first. The following sequence of events can begin to unlock a parish's generosity:

1. You figure out some way to find the money from outside sources to address the immediate crisis, and you get the work underway.

2. This relieves some of the acute anxiety that has kept people from seeing a future.

3. Because the money has come from outside, it makes the congregation realize that they are not alone, and that the rest of the church cares about them.

4. Resolving the immediate crisis gives you some credibility when you start to talk about other things that can happen. After all, you were right about the heating system; you could possibly be right about something else.

5. As the realization sinks in that the buildings they love can be restored, people begin to step forward with ideas, then with money, for projects that interest them.

REASONABLE DEBT
PLAYS A ROLE

Making a little progress causes additional progress to seem possible. Slowly at first, then with increasing speed, you find the parish able to address more of the needs of the buildings. In my experience taking on reasonable debt to address the immediate building crisis is appropriate, because the progress with the buildings, the articulation of a vision for the future, and the easing of interpersonal tensions leads to more money in the operating budget, so the loan can be repaid.

All this will not happen overnight. At Intercession we had to borrow about $100,000 for the heating system work. This was an interest-only line of credit from the diocesan office for three years that would then convert to a ten-year loan. Two years in, things still looked pretty bleak to me, though others kept telling me things were better. It seemed that all I had accomplished in that time was to put the parish deeper in debt. However, by the time it was necessary to begin paying principal and interest on the loan balance, we had developed the income streams necessary to support the loan.

Loans for capital purposes may not be the only borrowing needed. At Intercession I was faced immediately not only with the heating system work but will a turn-off notice from Con Ed because of arrears from the previous heating season. Our progress with the operating budget can be measured by how we paid Con Ed for the four heating seasons I was there. Weeks after I was sent to Intercession I told the bishop he needed to come up with $25,000 to pay the arrears or they would turn us off, which in my estimation would so demoralize the congregation that we would not be able to go on. He came through with the grant. The next winter we had to borrow $14,000 against the line of credit to pay one month's bill. The third winter we made it through with several special emergency appeals. The last winter we simply paid the bills with no particular pain.

At St. Mary's we needed to borrow only $14,500 from the diocesan office to get the roof job started in October 2010. Over the next few months people gave enough to pay the rest of the contractor's charges. The diocesan loan was completely repaid by August 2011.

I do not recommend profligate borrowing. One parish in a small upstate New York town embarked on building a new parish hall. They raised only a little over half of the $1.1 million needed, partly because the rector left during the capital campaign. Instead of getting the funding in place before construction, they got a balloon loan for the remainder from a local bank, and the interim oversaw construction. The new rector has to figure out how to deal with a debt equal to about two years' operating income. Fortunately, she is very competent, and the parish is enthusiastic and growing. With a combination of a second capital campaign and an increased operating budget, they are likely to be able to make it. However, I do not recommend that kind of borrowing—and most banks today will not let you do it anyway.

NOTE TO THE DIOCESE:
YOU HAVE TO HELP

At both Intercession and St. Mary's, at least part of the money needed to address the building crisis came from the diocesan office. If things are merely in decline, it may be enough to put in place the kind of leadership that can turn things around without diocesan cash. If the parish really is at the brink, however, the diocesan structures are going to have to be willing to make available the resources necessary to get things moving in the right direction. At both Intercession and St. Mary's my compensation came from funds at the discretion of the bishop. In both cases diocesan funds were required to begin to address the building crisis.

I was a consultant in another diocese where the bishop's office wanted a parish to be brought back from the brink but was not willing or able to put funds into it. The turnaround, unsurprisingly, did not happen, and the parish has closed. I was unable to convince them that a parish that had been allowed to decline ever since a bungled dispute in the late 1970s over the Prayer Book and women's ordina-tion was not going to fix itself with a congregation of sixteen and a supply priest. That's a lot like asking a roof to put its own new shingles on.

The analogy is apt, because allowing a parish to get to the brink is like defer-ring maintenance on a building: it costs more to get it back into shape than it would have if minor repairs had been made along the way. If a parish gets to the brink, it is always a failure of local leadership, but it is also always a sign that there has been a failure of leader-ship on the diocesan level. Sure, it would have been difficult to try to dis-lodge an arrogant, well-known rector who refused to leave, even though it was clear to three bishops that he was killing the parish. Sure, there are always other crises that demand attention. Sure, the main damage happened on your predecessor's watch. Neverthe-less, we are an episcopal church; the bishops in office cannot evade their responsibility for such situations or blame others. The bishops who de-scribe their role primarily as cheerleaders may not be apt choices for leadership when the gymnasiums in which the game is played have fallen into ruin. Something more, namely leadership, is required.

The point is that, if a substantial parish is sliding into the abyss, diocesan structures are complicit in its near-failure, and diocesan funds will almost certainly be required to help pull it out.

DEVELOP SOME KIND
OF CAPITAL PLAN

In addition to the initial crisis, every back-from-the-brink situation will have many building issues that need to be addressed. You need to get some kind of handle on what needs to be done and what the priorities are. Some things may be more pressing than others. Some jobs need to be done before others are done. For example, the envelope of the building needs to be sealed before you do interior finish work. If you can have a conditions survey done, that will be a great help. If yours is an historic building, depending on where you are, you might be able to get a grant to help cover the cost. Maybe the diocesan office can help.

You may very well need to go forward without a formal study of the conditions of the buildings. Often that is fine. You and others can see what you would like to have done, and you can train your eyes to see what needs to be done. Use a self-assessment tool that guides you in looking all around and noting things that need attention. Walk around with a small group so that several sets of eyes are looking. Discuss the results. The idea is not so much to come to an action decision that day as to begin to form a common list of things that need to be done now and things you would like to see done when possible in the future.

One relatively small item that often is neglected but should be fixed right away is the leader and gutter system. Perhaps the gutters are not being cleaned twice a year. Perhaps the leaders are not connected to the gutters or do not carry the water far enough from the foundation. These are relatively minor matters, but it is not always easy to tend to them. The gutters might be high off the ground; they might be historic and expensive to replace; they might be in out-of-the-way places. Because they are out of sight, they will tend to be out of mind. Keep harping on this until you figure out a way to deal with it. You will save the buildings from a lot of expensive damage if you keep the leaders and gutters properly cleaned and maintained.

LEARN ABOUT BUILDINGS

You may have taken courses that exposed you to architectural concepts, but the emphasis was probably on learning to recognize various styles by their components. You probably did not learn about the restoration, rehabilitation, and maintenance of historic buildings, but that is definitely part of the job of many priests who are in charge of congregations today.

Many clergy try to evade their responsibilities by entrusting building matters to one parishioner or an architect or contractor. This is a mistake, no matter how expert the trusted person. You cannot listen to just one voice and think you have done your job. It is necessary to hear a variety of opinions and figure out how best to go forward.

Here is an example. A colleague faced a complicated heating system job. He likes feeling certain that he is doing the "right" thing, and for him that usually means doing what some authority has said is the right thing. But he was in a quandary. Two experienced contractors had looked at the job. One said it was necessary to do a fairly expensive repair that the other contractor said was not warranted. He called me because he knew I had worked with both contractors. He was hoping I would say that one was more reliable than the other, so the ambiguity in his mind would be resolved. I told him that they were both reliable so it wasn't going to be that easy. He was going to have to repeat conversations with each one to learn why one was strongly in favor of doing something the other did not think was necessary. He was going to have to find other opinions as well. He was going to have to become more knowledgeable about this matter than he wanted to become, in order to help the vestry make a good decision.

Contractors, engineers, and architects, like doctors, lawyers, and priests, vary in their level of expertise on different aspects of their profession. You cannot simply rely on someone you like or someone you consider an authority. You have to learn enough about the issue to pick your way through the competing recommendations to the best course of action. There are lots of best practices in these matters, but there is no certainty, apart from these facts: first, this is part of your job; and second, these are important decisions with long consequences for ill and for good. Do not shortchange these matters.

LET OTHER THINGS HAPPEN
AS THEY CAN

If the buildings are not in a state of serious disrepair—if water isn't pouring in somewhere and the heating system is operable—start talking to people about what could be done to improve the physical condition and usage of the buildings. Encourage others to think and talk. People will be interested in different things. You do not want to control the discussions or even to guide them to certain projects. All you need to do is to make sure that, if the project requires parish money, there has been proper planning, good communication, and appropriate approvals.

Many of the ideas will go nowhere, at least at first. The money will not be available, or something else will have to be done first, or the community will not yet be ready for it, or what seemed manageable turns into a much bigger project. All that is all right, as long as you can communicate that the time will come when it can be done because we are moving in the right direction toward the future everyone wants to see happen.

You know your leadership is successfully implanting the idea that there is a future when people start to do things on their own. This will cause some problems. In a parish on the brink of failure people will be less concerned with solving problems than with staying in control, less interested in making things better than in maintaining their position. If in the spring someone beds out a flat of impatiens in a small area that had been covered with weeds, someone will no doubt complain, "Well, who does she think *she* is?" and

"Who gave her permission to do that?" Your job is to say thank you to the volunteer, to commiserate with her about what others are saying, and to say to the miffed, "I think they look great. It's much prettier than it was, isn't it? I think it's great that those weeds are gone." Your consistent message is that people are encouraged to offer what they can. Parish structures are meant not to stifle but to empower. The idea is to coordinate, not control.

The people will probably have little experience of coordination. They will not know how to talk with each other to come to a consensus, since their experiences have all been feeling sullen about decisions made by others. Every capital project is a chance to teach transparency and consensus-building. At Intercession, when we had received the funds to replace a twenty-five-foot dossal curtain behind the altar, I asked the maker to provide three or four samples of possible fabrics and trim. After each of the three services one Sunday I invited anyone who wished to stay after and discuss them. My own preference changed as a result of these conversations, and in the end we reached a general consensus. Those who did not get the style they preferred were quite happy, because they had been consulted, and they had been listened to.

As you are trying to get lay leaders to give up their unhealthy control, you need to make sure you are not filling the vacuum by controlling things yourself. This is a besetting problem of clergy generally and especially those with strong personalities. A donor offered to buy new choir vestments that the choir would choose. In that discussion they opted for something that reminded me of the Baptist church in which I was raised. I said a couple of times, "Are you sure you don't want cassock and cotta?" They were quite sure. Okay. It's not about what I prefer. And the cassock and cotta go back only to the nineteenth century. More importantly, I do not want people to bend to my wishes on things that concern them. I want to find what their preferences and passions are.

A parish on the brink is like a barren lot where nothing can grow in the compacted soil and everything that has tried to come up has been trampled down. Your work is to encourage any new shoot that appears and to soften the ground around it so it can grow better. Maybe you will find over time that the plant would do better in another part of the grounds. Okay. You can transplant it or even remove it later. Don't permit yourself or anyone else to prevent it from coming up now.

In time, if things go well, people will start to offer ideas and gifts that will let bigger things happen, and the time will be right. These will no doubt require contractors, maybe architects, careful bids and approvals. By that time people will be in a healthier place. They will have learned to say "thank you" instead of "who does he think *he* is?" And that will be because of your good leadership.

CHAPTER SEVEN

Make the Budget Work

Structural problems need structural solutions.
—Mohamed A. El-Erian, CEO of Pimco

*You won't get him
Thinkin' and a-prayin', wishin' and a-hopin'.*
—Wishin' and Hopin', Burt Bacharach

Congregations that are troubled or at the brink of closing always have a financial component contributing to their decline. In addition to whatever problems your buildings have, your operating budget will probably have a structural deficit or be underfunded. A structural deficit is different from a temporary lack of money. For example, many parishes experience decreased cash flow during the summer months. The third-quarter insurance and pension bills may not be able to be paid in July or August. However, when things pick up in the fall, people catch up on their pledges, cash flow improves, and the treasurer can breathe a little easier.

A structural deficit means that the identified sources of regular income are not sufficient to meet necessary expenses. Even if all the income targets are met, it will not be enough to support the operation. The structure of the budget is not sound. This cannot be fixed by one-time expedients, like using an unexpected bequest to pay the insurance bill. It also cannot be fixed by wishing and hoping. The structural problem remains and can be addressed only by a structural solution.

It is also possible for the budget to be balanced, but still underfunded. You can pay for what is in the budget, but your budget is insufficient to provide for a full-time priest, a secretary, or a sexton. And since you do not have the resources for these necessary operating items, you are almost certainly not setting funds aside in a capital reserve account to keep up with building maintenance, so you are borrowing from your buildings every year.

A healthy financial operation means at least these four things:

- The expense side of the budget provides for sufficient staff and the resources for a thriving operation.

- Sufficient revenue streams have been identified to fund that level of staff and resources, and the budget is realistically balanced.

- Seventy-five percent or more of the income in the operating budget comes from individual contributions.

- In addition to a healthy, realistic, balanced operating budget, another stream of regular, recurring income has been identified that goes directly into the capital reserve fund so that building maintenance is not deferred.

Some church leaders may add other considerations. For example, there are many who think the net proceeds from fundraising events like fairs and dinners should not be used in the operating budget, but rather should go to outreach or mission projects beyond the parish. And I believe it is dangerous for the operating budget to depend on any resources from investments. However, if 75 percent or more of your operating budget comes from pledge, plate, and other gifts, I would not quibble too much about where the other 25 percent comes from. I will try to persuade you, though, not to use income from investments in the operating budget.

GETTING FROM HERE
TO HEALTH

By these criteria very few parishes have a healthy financial operation. This does not mean the criteria are unreasonable; rather, it demonstrates how far we have permitted our parishes to go down paths that lead only to more decline and eventual death. Unless you are one of the rare financially sound congregations around today, there will almost certainly be a gap between the structure of your current budget and the healthy finances described above. Relatively few parishes receive three-quarters of their operating income from plate and pledge, and most that do are still seriously underfunded. Most parishes with long-term investments are overdrawing them to support the operating budget. Almost no parishes are reserving adequately for capital needs. And too many parishes have for so long been concerned with keeping a declining operation going that they have not thought for years or decades about the level of resources it would take to fund a thriving operation.

So the question is this: how can you begin to move from where you are to where you need to be to have a healthy, sustainable financial future?

With this question before you, the annual budget stops being an exercise in figuring out how you can make it through another year. Instead, it is an opportunity to project—realistically—the progress you will be able to make in the coming year toward a better financial condition.

This means that the leadership must begin to think about what a healthier financial condition would look like. You do not need a forty-year plan; you do not even need a five-year plan. You especially do not need a plan with unreasonable goals—for example, one that calls for doubling attendance in five years. Such a "plan" will lead only to recriminations and will reinforce the sense that nothing can be done.

You do need a sense of direction. You need to identify some concrete steps that can be taken right now that will incrementally improve the structure of the budget. How can we do a better job of soliciting pledges? How can we talk about money in a way that inspires people to be as generous as they have always wanted to be? How can we ratchet down the amount we are overspending from the endowment to get it to a sustainable level? How can this fundraising event be done better? Can we get a tenant for this space we are not using?

There will be disappointments. Perhaps you have a tenant organization that is in a stronger position than the parish. The outside organization knows the parish depends on the rent, and has been known to throw its weight around as a result. You are trying to develop new income streams, and you are, in a friendly, respectful but firm way, setting some boundaries with the tenant. The tenant may bolt because the organization realizes its control is jeopardized. The vestry is nervous about losing the income. You may have to figure out how to live without that rental income while you are finding a new and better tenant. Some may see this as a setback, but it is really part of the work of moving ahead.

You will not get there all at once. You may need to move laterally before you can move ahead. Or like a quarterback setting up a pass, you may need to take some steps backward without losing sight of how you want to move the game forward.

THERE ARE NO "BAD" SOURCES OF INCOME

There are sources of income that are healthier for the financial future of the parish than others, and there are sources of income that are more sustainable than others, but, as long as you are not involved in illegal activities, try not to attach moral value to the ways you can raise money to make the budget more in balance. For example, I agree that it is healthier in the long-term for the budget not to rely on fundraising events. However, I learned an important lesson from my father's mistake in the parish he was serving when I was born. He suppressed a strawberry festival that provided a fair percentage of the parish's income because he said, rightly, that the church should be supported by gifts from the members, not from a community event. The pledges for the next year could not bridge the gap created by the loss of revenue, however, and he was forced to backtrack because he had tried to go from Point A to Point M without the necessary interim steps. He also overlooked the value of the fellowship and camaraderie that came from everyone working together on a major initiative.

There may be party rentals or other income sources that you wish the parish did not depend on, but these things can all be dealt with in good time. *The one thing that must be stopped as quickly as possible is any overspending of the investments.* Every year you overspend the investments, it is as if you were selling a strip of property. You will never get that money back, and your successors in office will not thank you. If you have any sense that the parish has a future, you must stop overspending the investments as quickly as possible. We will discuss later in this chapter how to do that.

Many church leaders feel uncomfortable about trying to maximize rental income. Wouldn't it be better to make our spaces available at little or no cost to worthy projects and organizations? Well, of course it would. But it may be that you just cannot afford to do that right now. As you develop new revenue streams, you will be able to make spaces available at little or no cost to some users while asking market rents from others. In the meantime, it will not be helpful to the congregation if you beat yourself up about having to charge rent—or let your colleagues make you feel bad about it—while you are moving the budget to greater stability.

If you know that you are moving toward something better, you can allow yourself to pitch your tent for a time in places where you would not want to live permanently. For example, when we bought our current house, a friend removed and threw away the asphalt shingle under the front bay window, exposing the deteriorated clapboard beneath. He wanted to force us to undertake the exterior restoration right away. I knew we were a long way from being able to do the outside, so I took shingles from the roof we were putting on and covered up what my friend had uncovered. Those ugly roofing shingles stayed there for the next twenty-three years until we were ready to undertake the exterior restoration. I did not like it, but I knew that eventually we would get to the destination of a fully restored exterior, so I could put up with it.

If your budget is as structurally unsound as most, you may need the financial equivalent of scaffolding to support it, and sidewalk bridging to protect passersby, while you are rebuilding it. You may need to take advantage of expedients like rentals and fundraising events while the pledge and plate lines are becoming healthier and the investments are recovering.

It is okay to take detours if the main road is impassable. Don't waste time and energy trying to make sure that the budget is supported only by income sources you consider pure. You may not be the best judge of that, and your fixed ideas may permanently weaken the institution you are leading. In the 1920s John D. Rockefeller, Jr., a devout Northern Baptist, approached New York's Bishop William T. Manning with a gift of $500,000 toward the construction of the Cathedral of St. John the Divine and a request to be a trustee. "Although Rockefeller's gift was accepted, his application for board membership was refused,"[25] because he was not an Episcopalian. So Mr. Rockefeller turned his attention and his generosity, which might have completed the Cathedral, to the Riverside Church nearby, which was quickly built. The bishop's action was more rigid than principled. It was hardly visionary, and it did rather give the lie to the Cathedral's self-billing as "a house of prayer for all people." And when the

Cathedral is finished, it will not be according to the plan Bishop Manning envisioned.

Lottery winnings often are the object of principled scorn. I do not favor state-sponsored gambling. I think it is bad policy. It functions mostly as a regressive tax on the poor, and it does not seem to have hurt illegal gambling operations that much. One parishioner at Intercession said that she never hit the legal numbers anyway, but that she had raised her children on her winnings from the street numbers runners.

I have learned that gambling, like most things, looks different if the paths open to the white middle class are closed to you. That same parishioner, like my mother, had been widowed young with small children. They are all doing well, but she told my mother that she was most grateful for the fact that none had ever been jailed. Mother realized with shocked shame that she had never thought about giving thanks for that, since keeping white kids out of prison is not that difficult. Your position naturally shapes your point of view. For a while, until I actually started to make progress with Intercession's revenue streams, I bought lottery tickets twice a week, joking that the lottery was my Plan A for Intercession, and I was working to develop a Plan B. I now understand that my own disapproval of gambling is at least partly due to the fact that I have more control over the economic realities of my life than many others.

At a stewardship conference I was leading for one of the provinces of the Episcopal Church a participant asked heatedly if I would accept a donation that came from lottery winnings. I knew that his diocese had a long-standing policy discouraging raffles or other kinds of gambling at parish fundraisers and had recently devoted an entire issue of the diocesan newspaper to gambling, conveying the definite message that parishes should refuse gifts from that source. I also knew that this man thought that policy was foolish. He was testing me to see what kind of fool I might be. I said of course I would accept such a gift, adding that, since Episcopalians seem to be very unlucky, I doubted I would ever have the opportunity.

Be careful of having too many principles about where money comes from. God's ideas and instruments are often much less respectable than those we would have chosen. Part of what you are resisting in any turnaround situation is a system that is designed to produce failure, one that would rather fail than change. Rejecting a source of revenue because it is not your ideal is just a little too close for comfort to that approach.

PAPERING OVER
FINANCIAL PROBLEMS

It is an important part of your work to help people think openly, honestly, and clearly about parish finances. Most of us would rather not confront evidence at every vestry meeting of how far our parish is from financial health, so most parishes, without any discussion or conscious decision, have figured out ways to hide the problem. Your parish got to the edge of the abyss in part because information was not shared, and clear thinking about money was not encouraged. Setting up good budgeting procedures and making available complete and clearly organized reports are important aspects of your work. Again, you may not be able to get there all at once. It took me three years at Intercession to get regular monthly reports to the vestry.

Years ago I was looking at the budget of a congregation that has been an aided mission for almost all of its 135 years. The budget showed $19,000 of solid income that could be expected from pledge, plate, fundraising, and space use income. The expense side listed $91,000 of expenses. I was inexperienced, so I was more or less speechless. The vestry was not concerned because they knew that, in the end, they would have about $19,000 in income, and they would spend about the same amount. They did not consider an unbalanced budget to be a problem, because they did not think that budgeting was important. Probably someone from the diocesan office had told them it was important to have a budget, so they went through an annual exercise that meant nothing to them while continuing to operate as they always had.

Adopting a realistic budget is one of the vestry's more important governance functions. Failing to adopt a realistic budget is a failure of vision as well as a failure of fiduciary responsibility. Monthly reports need to have budget comparisons. If the budget is seen as unimportant or unrelated to the operation of the parish, the vestry understands neither its governance role nor its leadership function. It goes without saying that a parish near the brink of failure will have lost sight of both.

The purpose of a budget is to provide a road map for the progress you intend to make in the current year. It sets targets for the various income streams. Those involved in raising funds from those sources of income then know what they have to do. The budget also authorizes expenditures at certain levels. You do not have to seek vestry approval for budgeted items because the vestry authorized those expenses in adopting the budget. It is necessary to have the vestry's approval to overspend a budget line or to spend money for something not included in the budget.

If you adopt a budget that is not realistically balanced, it simply means that you have postponed decisions that will need to be made before the end of the year. If the budget is within a few percentage points of being balanced, I suppose the leadership's hope might be that some income lines might be a little higher and some expense lines a little lower. That is a wish, however, not a plan. Some might want to make sure there is always a deficit so people will feel under the gun and anxious to make it up. Generally this strategy is urged by someone with some serious control needs. Control and anxiety are not the tools of good leadership, and it is smarter not to use them.

At a recent conference a priest said the lay leadership in the parish she serves always budgets a deficit as a statement of faith and that every year the deficit gets met as some lines come in over the amount budgeted. I suggested that they look back at the last few years and see what income lines they have been underbudgeting, and bring them up to more honest levels. A realistically balanced budget is not evidence of a lack of faith. And it is always okay to end the year with a surplus.

If the budget is out of balance by less than ten percent of projected income, you might as well figure it out and make the tough decisions now rather than later. If the budget is out by more than ten percent, you really need some fresh thinking. If it is that far out of balance, it isn't really a budget because it does not provide a useful road map for the next year. When income cannot cover budgeted expenses, what is such a budget actually authorizing anyone to spend money on?

Maybe you say that the deficit will be made up by previous years' accumulated operating surpluses. There might be a situation in which that idea makes sense, but if it exists, it is rare. By using operating reserves this year, you are building in a problem for next year's budget. It's like withdrawing money from your retirement savings to pay your property taxes this year. How will you pay them next year?

Having a budget that is wildly out of balance actually does hide the problem in plain sight. Everybody sees it, but probably nobody will ask about it because the problem appears too daunting. New vestry members may think that those who have been around longer know what they're doing. The elephant sits in the middle of the room, but people somehow get used to ignoring it.

In order to be useful, the budget must be realistically balanced.

MISPLACED FAITH,
UNREALISTIC PROJECTIONS

Another way to pretend that there is no problem is to make unrealistic projections on the income and expense sides of the budget. Income lines are raised to levels that cannot reasonably be achieved, and expense lines are budgeted unrealistically low. This is frequently presented as a "challenge" or a "faith" budget, but it is usually just another way of putting off difficult decisions because the budget is actually not balanced.

One bishop, saying that she operated out of abundance, would shut down any discussion of financial realities and belittle those concerns as petty and negative. In point of fact, dealing with reality is the faithful approach; trying to pretend that reality is other than it is betrays a lack of trust in the God who created and works through the real world. You do not need an MBA to turn a parish around, but you will not succeed if you refuse to address the financial situation realistically. It is possible to make progress toward the vision of a healthy financial future only by addressing present realities and making plans that can be implemented step by step to make the future reality better. If the clergy and vestry are intimidated by numbers or do not understand the budget, they need to have the humility and strength necessary freely to acknowledge their weaknesses in this regard, and to learn from those who know more. Being realistic and smart about money matters does not mean we are faithless or refusing to place our trust in God to provide.

The budget projections and actual performance need to be kept close together. I have seen a number of finance committees try to put the following year's budget together by looking only at previous budgets. And many vestries receive reports only on actual results without reference to the budget.

When developing the budget for next year, you need before you the following:

- ⚱ the previous year's actual results, and perhaps the actual results of the year before the previous year;

- ⚱ the current year actual results to date; and

- ⚱ the current year budget.

You do not need the budgets from previous years, only the actual results. Your budget deliberations need to know what actually happened in previous years, not what you thought would happen. And four columns of numbers are about all that anyone can take in. The usefulness of the entire document diminishes with every additional column.

HIDING NUMBERS IN THE BUDGET

One way to keep financial reports from being useful is by failing to organize the information in ways that would promote understanding. There needs to be the right information, the appropriate level of detail, an appropriate formatting of income and expense categories, sufficient context to understand, and clarity in presentation.

Many parishes present reports from low-end accounting software packages that alphabetize revenue and expense categories. Because the expenses for the copier, office supplies, postage, and telephone are separated by other items, you cannot get a sense of what it costs to operate the office. You need to pull together like items into subtotaled groupings. This will require using numbers, at least for the general headings, such as Personnel, Program Expenses, Office Expenses, Plant Operating Expenses, and so on, so the groups appear in the order you want. This grouping is important, because you want to help the leadership think in broad terms about how much of the budget comes from individual contributions, and how much it costs to operate various aspects of parish life. Grouping like income and expenses items with bolded subtotals encourages people to understand the big picture.

The appropriate level of detail is tricky. You want to give complete information, but you do not want a jumble of little numbers, and you do not want the report to exceed two pages. Information needs to be complete, but appropriately summarized. For example, people may have envelopes for major festivals as well as every saint's day, but it is wrong-headed to list every feast day on the financial report for the vestry. List Easter and Christmas separately, and group the others together under "Other Holy Days." If an income or expense line is less than one or two percent of the budget, it probably does not need a separate line. People will gravitate toward discussing the smallest numbers in a financial report because they are the least threatening numbers to discuss. Provide complete information, but do not give unimportant numbers. The fact that the Twelve Step group is giving you $20 a week instead of $25 just isn't important enough for a twenty-minute discussion at a vestry meeting. Let the finance committee or the priest and the officers work on that. What AA gives you should be grouped with other incidental rental income under "Other Space Use Income."

Of course the treasurer should be prepared and have more detail with her so that if a question comes up about a particular line, she can answer the question on the spot. It hinders the building of trust to have to say you'll get back to people. That's the dynamic that leads vestry members to think that someone is hiding something. Then they demand reports that list the offering for every saint's day. And then the discussions descend once again to a level that is simply unhelpful and unproductive.

Often financial reports do not give the appropriate context so people can use them well. The questions the vestry needs to deal with are these:

- How are we doing so far this year?

- How does that compare with where we thought we would be?

- How are we doing compared to last year?

- What are our targets for the year?

In order to answer these questions you need the following columns in the reports:

- current year-to-date actual results;

- current year-to-date budget numbers;

- the previous year's actual results, to date; and

- the total current year budget.

If any of these columns are lacking, the report will not have the appropriate context. If you include additional columns, you will decrease the usefulness of the report. People generally cannot deal with more than four columns of numbers or with reports that are longer than two pages. You do not need columns for percentages or variances. Your eye will do that as you read across the columns.

The budget lines concerning investment income can often be formatted in such a way as to hide uncomfortable financial realities when a parish is overspending their investments as well. I have seen reports where there is an income line called "Investment Income." Then there is another line that represents the amount in excess of the first number that the vestry has decided to withdraw to plug budgeted deficits. And then the financial report shows a deficit. When you ask what is funding the deficit, people say,

"Oh, it comes from the investments." So the total being taken from the investments is disguised because it appears in three places, and one of the three numbers is implicit, not clearly stated. When this is happening, you can be pretty sure that no one is thinking about the draw from the investments in terms of a sustainable percentage. People are just withdrawing what it takes to plug the hole.

This way of hiding the overspending of the investment income of the parish will be a mistake in the long run. It is much smarter to be transparent. If you are using resources from your investments to support the operating budget, here are two practices I suggest you adopt. First, show the entire amount you are taking from the investments in one place, so people are aware of the total number. And second, be sure you know what percentage of a three-year average the total taken from the investments represents.

The treasurer should be prepared to say, "This $70,000 represents ten percent of a three-year moving average. A sustainable percentage is four to five percent."

THE SHAPE OF THE BUDGET

What I have said about budgeting and reporting may seem like petty concerns, but these are important matters. There are two main reasons why people do not understand the parish's finances and cannot think about them clearly. Either they are not being given the proper information, or the information they receive is not presented in a way that encourages understanding. People need information that is appropriately organized so they can think clearly about the situation.

The reason I have insisted on reports that contain certain information presented in certain ways is that in my experience this is the way to start getting the vestry to think in terms of the shape of the parish's finances. What kind of shape does a healthy budget have?

We will look first at the income side. There are only four sources of operating income for parishes, apart from diocesan assistance:

§ individual gifts;

§ rentals;

§ fundraising events;

§ resources from investments.

Despite the fond wishes of some vestry members, there simply are no other ways to get money for the basic operation of the church. There are sometimes private and public grants available, but they are almost always for capital work or outreach programs. Your operating budget has to come from the four sources cited above.

I have listed them in the order I think they should be used to support the budget. Individual gifts—that is, pledge, plate, and other contributions—make up about 75 percent or more of a healthy operating budget. There can be no financial health without a consistent and effective effort to do stewardship formation and institutional fundraising that increases the percentage of operating income from this source. Stewardship formation is getting people to see themselves as stewards, not owners, of what they have. In financial terms that means modeling and commending tithing or proportional giving off the top. Institutional fundraising is the work all not-for-profits must do to make the case to potential donors that they are worthy recipients of their constituents' contributions. Even if all your members were tithing, you would still have to do a good job of showing them why all or part of their tithe should go to you.[26]

Rentals are the second-best way to fund the budget. A great deal of your budget goes to the maintenance and operation of the physical plant. If there are spaces available, it makes sense for the buildings to generate all the revenue they can.

Fundraising events, the third way to generate income, are good for the life of the parish as well as the financial bottom line. When I consult with a parish that runs no fundraising events, I see a vitality problem. Fellowship and community are built when the congregation works together on several efforts each year to raise funds. Fundraisers can present difficulties when they are used to support the operating budget. In many congregations a frantic round of fundraising events is needed because the pledge drives are ineffective. Fairs and penny socials are no substitute for good annual giving campaigns. However, using the proceeds of fundraising events to support the budget is preferable to using any funds from the investments to support the operating budget.

My recommendation for investment income is simple: *no income from the long-term investments should go into the operating budget.* If your budget is supported by the investments, you will almost certainly begin to overdraw the investments; that is, you will begin to use more than the four to five percent that can be spent over the long term from a properly diversified portfolio. If you have an endowment or long-term investments, wean the operating budget from its dependence on the investments, and use the drawdown from the investments to help fund your capital reserve.

So a healthy budget receives around 75 percent of the income from individual gifts, 15 to 25 percent from rentals and maybe up to ten percent from fundraising events. The goal is to have no income from investments funding the operating budget.

On the expense side, the components of the budget are:

- ᕔ *Total cost of all personnel:* lay and ordained, wages, salaries, and all benefits;

- ᕔ *Building maintenance and operation:* including utilities, insurance, maintenance and supplies, but not including staff costs, which are in the first part;

- ᕔ *Program:* by which I mean everything else, including Christian education, liturgical supplies, outreach, diocesan assessment, and the operation of the office, which is an important part of the parish's ministry and program.

There is no standard shape of the expense side, because much depends on the size of the buildings relative to the size of the budget, but I will say that the following are typically indicators of financial stress or chronic underfunding. These are analytical, not diagnostic, observations. They are not meant to judge, but to help you understand your current condition. You are probably experiencing stress if:

- ᕔ The cost of your cleric plus the diocesan assessment is more than 50 percent of operating income. This means you cannot afford the other staff you need. It probably also means that the buildings are eating up the other half of the budget.

- ᕔ You spend less than 50 percent of your budget on personnel, ordained and lay. Not-for-profits should spend a great deal on staff; the members of the staff are the people who deliver the services and accomplish the mission—not alone, of course, but their work supports, facilitates, and empowers volunteers. If you cannot afford to spend half your budget on personnel, it probably means the buildings demand too much.

- ᕔ The cost of operating the buildings is more than 25 percent of your budget.

⑤ Your average Sunday attendance at all services is less than 40 percent of your seating capacity.

From my experience of looking at parish budgets of all kinds, I will venture to say that a healthy budget means that the cost of adequate staffing is 55 to 60 percent, building costs are around 20 to 25 percent, and 20 to 25 percent is spent on program costs. This assumes that you are adequately funding the capital reserve from a regular recurring stream of income that does not go through the operating budget.

The purpose of these observations, again, is not to provide rigid standards, but rather to get your leadership thinking in terms of the shape of the current budget so that they can begin thinking about how to make progress toward a healthier, more sustainable shape.

THE SOLUTION IS ALWAYS ON THE INCOME SIDE

If you are in a situation that requires any kind of turnaround, keep in mind that over the mid- to long-term, the solution to any budget problem lies in increasing revenue, not in reducing expenses. Most parishes do not spend money on frills. On the contrary, in many places so much effort has gone into cutting expenses over the years that necessary and urgent matters are not included in the budget at all. Not only is there no fat; muscle and bone have been cut out, and perhaps limbs have been amputated.

Here are some expedients I have encountered. The vestry in one parish gave the women's group responsibility for providing altar supplies and flowers, and the choir was told that they needed to raise any funds required for music and vestments. In another, the members were told that if they wanted garbage bags or toilet paper and paper towels in the bathrooms, they needed to donate those supplies. So in a desperate effort to acquiesce to decline, these vestries stopped taking responsibility for worship and basic building maintenance.

No good leader takes a parish down such a road, because there is no future in that direction. Unless you see closing the parish as the only option, you will want to do something else, and the something else always has to do with figuring out how to increase existing sources of revenue and how to develop new income streams. It's not as easy as saying, "where there's a will, there's a way," but it is certainly true that if you do not believe a way exists, you will not find it.

Unless all your members are already tithing, you can increase individual giving. When I hear, as I hear at every parish I meet with, "You can't ask people in this parish to give more; they're all on fixed incomes," it tells me several things. First, leaders who say that do not intend to give more themselves. Second, the leadership has bought the notion that there's nothing that can be done. Third, the ways the leadership has tried to increase giving have been ineffective, probably because they have focused on budgets, obligation, and guilt. Finally, it tells me that the leadership is not practicing proportional giving off the top. Tithers don't think that way. I am one of four children raised by a widow on a very fixed income who tithed and taught us to tithe, so I know that the assertion that people cannot be asked to give more is defeatist, probably lazy, and simply untrue. You *can* increase individual giving. However, it means asking people to support the credible vision of the future that you have begun to outline, and it means asking in the ways that are effective. And it means being able to share with people your experience of proportional giving; it does not mean telling people they should do something you are not doing.

In the right circumstances a matching fund can be a way of jumpstarting individual giving. Here's how it worked in the mid-1990s at a major parish that was then on the ropes. At the time 350 pledges were producing $450,000. These may not seem like dire numbers, but the enormous plant is in the heart of midtown Manhattan. And the average pledge from this wealthy congregation was an anemic $1,300. The rector and the finance officer, later joined by the treasurer, each agreed to give an additional $10,000 in the following year. The extra $30,000 amounted to about seven percent of the total then being pledged. They asked the vestry to add another $70,000 so a challenge gift of $100,000 could be presented to the congregation. It took a while to get every vestry member on board, but when the challenge was presented, the congregation matched it two to one, and the total amount pledged rose to $750,000. A second challenge the following year led total pledges to rise to $1 million.

The challenge worked only because, first, the rector had been concentrating on stewardship formation throughout the period, and second, the leadership was articulating a compelling vision for the future that people wanted to be part of. If the pitch had been, "Give more so the doors can stay open another year," it would not have been effective.

You can probably also derive more revenue from the use of your buildings. Many options are available to you, if you can learn to see them; real estate is local, and each parish's facilities are different. However, if there are spaces built to be used for education and socializing, and if those spaces are not fully used for parish life, chances are you can figure out ways to offer them for use by outsiders. Do not simply concede defeat. Instead, try this:

§ Look. What are other people's spaces being used for?

§ Talk. Mention to everyone in the congregation and in the community that you are looking for different ways to use your space.

§ Listen. What kinds of spaces are people looking for and for what purposes?

§ Think. What kinds of needs are not being met in your community? What uses would your spaces lend themselves to?

§ Act. Follow up on any ideas that you have had or that others have offered.

It is not easy to be a landlord, and tellingly, churches are often not good at customer service. It is part of the "take it or leave it" way we present ourselves that I discussed in chapter 1. A friend tried to arrange a wedding reception through the hospitality operation of one of our seminaries. He tried to find out if the seminary chapel would be available for the ceremony. No answer ever came. He asked for a reduction in the room rate because he would be guaranteeing ten rooms for two nights. The answer was no. He asked if he could serve wines from his native South Africa. He would buy them, bring them, and pay a corkage fee. When the answer to that was no, he went to an establishment that actually wanted the business. Similarly, at both Intercession and at St. Mary's, the vestry said it wanted to rent the hall for private events, but then tried to set up obstacles that would have made it unlikely that anyone would want to use the spaces.

If you want to derive revenue from others' use of your spaces, be prepared to provide the kind of welcome and services you would expect if you were the prospective tenant. You have to think things through so you charge enough to cover all your overhead costs, which might, in some instances include property taxes, and you have to look at things from the point of view of the prospective tenant or user. For example, if the spaces will be used in the evenings, is the outdoor lighting sufficient? There is a discussion of these matters in one of my earlier books, *Remember the Future*.[27]

HOW TO STOP OVERSPENDING THE INVESTMENTS

A close friend came to a beautiful parish that had come into more money than they knew how to handle, and he saw that he had about four years to stop overspending the investments. That has been constantly on his mind, while he has rebuilt the education and formation program, begun new outreach ministries, brought to completion a large organ project, and visited all who have gone to the hospital within hours of their arrival. He's just about done it. There was no magic; there was just the constant, relentless pushing in every way he could come up with to raise other income streams and keep spending controlled so the investments could be preserved.

There are two reasons generally that investments come to be overspent. The first is that investment income used in support of the operating budget (not capital spending) will depress individual giving. Members figure they do not have to give because someone else's money will pay for the level of church life they want, and so there is more pressure every year to overdraw the investments to supplement the budget. This does not mean the members are uncommitted or faithless; rather, it means the leadership has mishandled having long-term investments.

Here's an example. The members of one lovely church had exemplary personal giving. They were dedicated, committed, and worked together. There wasn't really enough money, to be sure, but this urban, "pink collar" congregation had one of the highest average pledges in the diocese. Then, having just called a rector with a well developed sense of entitlement, they received a $2 million bequest from a long-time member. Within ten years two-thirds of the money was gone. The dollar amount pledged was down 30 percent from the year before the bequest came in. They had to get rid of the priest, who had become completely unaccountable. They are now known as a very fractious congregation. The bequest was not the problem. Bad leadership was the problem.

Second, investments used in support of the operating budget begin to
get overspent because of downturns in the market. Say a parish with $2
million invested in an appropriately diversified portfolio is taking a prudent
five percent, or $100,000, into the operating budget, and, like most
parishes, they are not funding a capital reserve fund.

The market declines for two years, and the portfolio loses 25 percent
of its value. Now the investments are worth about $1.5 million. The five
percent draw produces only $75,000. Rather than cut the budget, the
vestry decides to continue to draw $100,000. Actually, they decide to draw
$120,000 because of an unexpected building repair. Drawing out
$100,000 from $2 million is a sustainable five percent. Taking $120,000
from $1.5 million is an unsustainable eight percent.

The vestry promises themselves that the extra $20,000 is a one-time
borrowing that they will pay back. They may even enter the interfund
payable and receivable into the accounting system. The investments recover
somewhat, but the next year they need to replace some expensive valves
and piping in the boiler system. They continue to draw $100,000 into the
operating budget, and they take out $25,000 for the heating system work.

That's it. The habit is fully formed. Every year thereafter there will be
what appear to be compelling reasons to continue to take too much from
the investments. Without a change in leadership that parish will almost
certainly continue to overdraw the investments until they are depleted.

In sum, there are two reasons investments get overdrawn, and they are
both the result of poor leadership. Either the leadership does an inadequate
job of stewardship formation and institutional fundraising and people do
not give, or the leadership decides to overdraw the investments "just this
once," because of the "extraordinary circumstances we face this year."

It is very difficult to stop overspending investments. The leadership that
began the overspending will probably not be able to stop it. Overspending
will only reinforce, not reverse, the lack of vision that led to the decision
to overspend in the first place. If the priest is paying attention, she may
see that the trend is unsustainable, but figures that there is enough to see
her out. I have, unfortunately, seen numerous clergy, male and female,
make that cynical calculation. Some have retired just as the investments
neared zero; others made a judicious move to a parish that still had investments to spend down, proving, among other things, that the kind of reference checks search committees do might not tell them everything they
should know.

Let's say you are that new leader who can make a change in this pattern.
You must do at least several things simultaneously. First, you must begin

to communicate how important it is for the future of the parish to stop overspending. Second, you must be the voice that puts a constant brake on spending until existing revenue streams have been increased or new income streams found. Third, you must increase and find those sources of revenue. Here are the steps.

Step 1

When people are accustomed to overdrawing the investments, they stop thinking of the percentage they are taking out; they just take out what they think they need. The first step to getting control of the situation is to *calculate the total you are taking out as a percentage of a three-year average.* Total up everything you are taking out and figure it as a percentage of a three-year average. If you want to use some other average—a thirteen quarter average, or a thirty-six-month average—you can; just calculate what you are taking out as a percentage of some trailing average.

It does not matter whether you are taking money out for operating or capital purposes. People might have the idea that they can overdraw the investments for capital purposes. This is a mistake. You are taking what should be a permanent asset—the principal of the investments adjusted for inflation—and turning it into a depreciable asset—the buildings. I have heard very sophisticated investment guys say, "We're overspending the investments to invest in air conditioning the church." I said, "What exactly is going to be the return on that investment?" There was only a plan to spend; there was no plan to get a return from the "investment." You have to think straight. Don't let the language you use fool you into thinking that you are making an "investment" when what you are doing is simply overspending with no thought of how that money will ever be replaced. Let me be clear: I approve of air conditioning churches and doing other needed improvements; however, such work should not be funded from overspending the investments. Run a capital campaign instead.

What was your emotional reaction just now when I suggested a capital campaign? If you felt a negative surge that felt like, "Oh, we can't do that," or "That sounds like a lot of work," you are right now part of the problem and need to do some work to be an effective leader in your congregation. If you felt some enthusiasm and something like shackles coming undone, you are the kind of leader who can help your congregation get its investment spending under control.

Step 2

Next, *start ratcheting down the percentage to get to a sustainable draw.* If what you are taking out now works out to nine percent of the three-year average, then reduce your draw every year by one percent, or at least by one-half of one percent. For example, if the amount you are withdrawing this year comes to 9.5 percent, make next year's draw 9 or 8.5 percent. When you are making the budget for the next year, recalculate the trailing average and multiply it by 8.5 percent. That is all the income that is going to come from the investments for any purpose whatsoever. Make the budget work with that number. In the immediate term that may mean cutting spending while you work to develop other sources of revenue—increased individual giving, space use income, and fundraising events.

Step 3

This means that the third step is to get people to *think of the investment draw as one more limited income stream.* Every other source of revenue in your budget is limited in terms of what it can reasonably be expected to produce right now. You know you cannot just raise any one of the other sources of income you have to what it takes to balance your budget. You can't say, "Well, we'll just budget $50,000 more in pledges next year," or "We'll tell the nursery school to pay us twice as much next year." The investments will not protest, as would your members or your tenants, if you take far more from them than they can or want to pay. That discipline has to come from you. That is why it is so difficult.

There will be people who, for various reasons, simply will not understand why you are trying to get the draw down to a sustainable level. They will say, "Well, we *need* to fix the gutters," or "We *need* a full-time sexton." And this is true. The buildings need to be tended to, and the parish needs an appropriate level of staffing. When people say this, it means their thinking has been frozen; they can think of getting the money these things require only from the investments. The point is to get people to think about other places to get the money. Maybe you need a capital campaign for the building work. Maybe there's a way of producing additional revenue from the buildings that will pay for the staffing.

Step 4

So the fourth thing you need to do—and it is a very difficult indeed—is to *encourage people to think about where they would get the money the parish needs if they didn't have the investments.* Where would people get the money to fix the gutters or employ a full-time sexton if there were no endowment?

This will lead you to look more closely at the other possible sources of income discussed above.

There are no magic bullets here. This is a hard slog. The longer the parish has been overspending the investments the greater the resistance will be to getting control of the situation. Through all of the difficulties you will encounter in getting the investment draw to a sustainable level you will have to remember that you are doing something that is tough in the short run but necessary for long-term health of the institution, and something for which your successors, if competent, will be very grateful. And I hope you find that this will be satisfaction enough.

CHAPTER EIGHT

Healthy Leadership in a Post-Christendom Church

An undisciplined king ruins his people, but a city becomes
fit to live in through the understanding of its rulers.
— ECCLESIASTICUS 10:3

When you do something, you should burn yourself completely,
like a good bonfire, leaving no trace of yourself.
—SHUNRYU SUZUKI, ZEN PRIEST

So far we have discussed how the social context for the church has changed in a post-Christendom world. We have noted how our institutional DNA is still encoded with the approaches that worked when religion and culture had closer ties. We have examined the conventional wisdom that tries to justify our failure of leadership. We have treated at length the kinds of things you need to bring with you into a turnaround situation and how to get started. We have discussed how to get the buildings under control, and we have looked at the budget in ways that make it a tool for exercising financial leadership.

In this chapter we will look at the interpersonal dynamics of healthy leadership. I have referenced them many times in preceding chapters because you cannot (or should not) do anything all by yourself in any parish context. Other people are always involved. My intention here is to address the relational aspects of situations you will surely encounter, and how to deal with them *as a leader.* In addition, and just as importantly, I want to think about how to deal with them as the leader of a religious institution in a time when "the spiritual as such is no longer intrinsically related to society."[28]

REMEMBER: THE PEOPLE ARE PART OF THE SOLUTION

At a meeting I recently attended it was pointed out that "conflict over *leadership* and conflict over *finances* were the areas most strongly related to decline in average Sunday attendance."[29] In other words, conflict is often a symptom that there is a leadership problem. In response, several of the participants in the meeting said this information made them want to learn more about how to manage conflict. No one said that the information made them want to address the leadership problems that cause conflict. This reaction is completely in line with what I have observed in other contexts. There is a large cottage industry in the church of consultants to help people manage conflict. I haven't noticed that these efforts have been very successful. By the time a consultant is called in, it is usually too late to deal with the conflict in any way other than by the departure of the pastor or of a good part of the congregation, or usually both. And, of course, treating symptoms is unlikely to cure the underlying condition.

Most discussions of interpersonal relationships in parishes have to do with conflict. This is not surprising, because declining congregations in a declining church are convulsed with conflict. Declining congregations tend to have more conflict and more serious conflicts. Conflict and conflict resolution will not be the focus of this discussion, but I think it is useful to stake out a position on the subject.

There are at least two very different approaches in the literature on congregational conflict. There is the family systems approach pioneered by Edwin Friedman in his classic *Generation to Generation,* and elaborated by such books as *Never Call Them Jerks* by Arthur Paul Boers.[30] Such a view sees parish conflict as an expression of a lack of health in the system of interpersonal relationships, not the fault of one or more individuals. The leader's job, in Friedman's words, is to be differentiated and stay connected. Staying differentiated means managing your own feelings and reactions so you do not let yourself become enmeshed in the unhealthy dynamics of the community, but you also stay connected with all the players in the system. The thesis is that this makes the system healthier, which causes the ways people in the system relate to one another to become healthier. Much conflict is avoided because the leader refuses to engage in the dysfunction, yet maintains relationships with all the parties. The conflict that arises with such a leader will be the reaction of people whose power or position depends on the congregational system remaining unhealthy.

A very different, indeed incompatible, approach locates the problem in certain individuals in the congregation. Such books as *Clergy Killers* and *Antagonists in the Church* take scant notice of the interpersonal dynamics, but are predicated on labeling certain people as the problem and then move rather quickly to the language of spiritual warfare and exorcism.[31] Without the exorcism language, *When Sheep Attack!* still basically locates the problem in a small group who inexplicably want to get rid of a stellar pastor.[32]

While recognizing that people with severe mental disorders do exist and can be part of a congregation, and while acknowledging that you will frequently feel that your problems are being caused by such individuals, I

maintain that Friedman's approach is the more effective one. It is simply unhelpful, and rather arrogant, to locate the problem in one or more of the people. Years ago a friend who had spent her ordained ministry as a therapist began work at a small parish with a history of bad leadership and many problems. My friend said she was going to treat the congregation as clients who needed therapy. My partner and I were being knocked around in our turnaround situation, and her approach seemed like a good idea. However, her ministry there was much briefer and more tumultuous than she supposed it was going to be. If you think you are healthy and everyone around you is sick, it will be impossible for you to establish truly mutual relationships. You will not even want to. The people of our friend's parish were offended to be treated that way—and they were right. It simply does not work to approach parish ministry as if you are the healthy professional and all the members are sick.

Viewing other individuals as the problem will almost certainly set you up to be their victim. That may give you a way of feeling justified within yourself if things get really bad, but it is not a way to address the situation and get things to a healthier place. It will be difficult—and I freely admit that in the midst of people acting out it will sometimes be impossible; you will make mistakes, and you may be badly hurt (I can show you my scars). Yet for a successful turnaround to take place it is necessary to see the people as part of the solution, not as part of the problem.

The parish is not at the brink because of the people. The primary thesis of this book is that if the parish has reached the edge of the abyss, there has been a leadership failure, likely over a period of years, possibly involving more than one pastor, and probably abetted, or at least permitted to continue, by the diocesan office. Many clergy and bishops will want to resist this thesis because it is difficult to admit one's responsibility for a failed and wrong-headed effort. However, such resistance simply makes it more likely that ordained leaders will continue to act in similar ways while expecting different results. The point is that anything that encourages you to blame the people for the situation is not going to help turn the situation around.

This doesn't mean that the people do not need to change. In any on-the-precipice situation I have seen, the way people relate to one another in the system needs lots of work. People are mistrustful and cliquish, disdainful of others, secretive, and prone to snap one another's heads off. They will probably treat you the same way when you arrive. However, it is often a mistake to address those dynamics directly; people who believe their beloved parish is tanking simply cannot find the energy or wherewithal to be nicer to you and to each other in the face of such stress and grief. To a significant extent those dynamics will begin to correct themselves as the situation with the buildings and the budget get better, and as people see that you remain trustworthy and forbearing in the maelstrom.

DIFFICULT THINGS DO NOT REQUIRE CONFLICT

If it is true that ineffective leadership is a principal cause of conflict, then there might be more effective ways we can lead that will not lead to conflict. I do not mean avoiding conflict in the bad sense of allowing people to act with no accountability. I mean leading in ways that keep the community on the road to health without falling into the conflicts that result from maladroit or self-centered leadership. Of course situations arise where some difficult thing must be done. If it is done badly, it could lead to serious conflict. There probably are, however, other ways of doing it that will allow something more positive to happen.

I said in the first chapter that I do not believe the adoption of the 1979 *Book of Common Prayer* is a cause of the decline of the Episcopal Church. I will now nuance that assertion by saying that *the way it was introduced* led directly to the decline of many parishes. The Prayer Book was not the problem; however, the way the leadership dealt with the need to bring it into use in every parish was frequently a problem.

The 1979 book did not call only for minor changes in some of the prayers and rites, as had the 1892 and 1928 revisions. The signal accomplishments of the current Prayer Book were the restructuring of the eucharistic rite and the achievement of the sixteenth-century English reformers' goal of the Eucharist as the principal Sunday service, after more than four hundred years of that service being Morning Prayer in most congregations, with the Great Litany and Ante-Communion.

Here are two examples of how the leadership bungled the introduction of the new rites in ways that seriously weakened the parishes involved.

In one parish a rector called in 1981 made the switch from Morning Prayer to the Eucharist on the first Sunday he arrived. There was, of course, a furor in that self-consciously Morning Prayer parish. He was adamant and defensive; many left; and his ministry—which continued there for many years—never recovered. During his twenty-five years at the parish he did everything in the same high-handed manner he had used to change the parish's liturgical practice. The parish, a substantial plant in a large suburban downtown, may well not survive.

In another parish the rector wanted nothing to do with any changes to the 1928 Prayer Book. He never introduced the 1979 book at all and in effect made devotion to the old book a litmus test for membership in the parish for the next twenty years. More than a decade after his retirement, and after two brief, failed rectorates, that parish, considerably smaller than it was, finally has the prospect of being rebuilt.

Here's how it could have gone. My partner John went to a resolutely low-church Morning Prayer parish in 1982 and made incremental changes in introducing the Eucharist over seven years, while working to rebuild a failing congregation. Not a single person left over the change, even though there were many who missed Morning Prayer as it gradually, then finally, disappeared. Everyone knew where he was going, but he listened, he took people's opinions into account, and he paid attention to how people felt. Significantly, he did not expect those who did not want the change to believe that the Eucharist was the only theologically correct worship on Sunday morning; rather, they could simply accept that since the church was moving in this direction, the parish needed to move that way as well. The life, he repeatedly said, is in the mainstream, not in the stagnant pools at the margins. His patent good will and love for the parish and its people were major reasons for the lack of conflict over the biggest liturgical change in the parish's history. This is an example of the method I believe is effective in dealing with difficult issues.

Of course John had to deal with the snide remarks of some colleagues who congratulated themselves on making the change more expeditiously, despite unpleasant consequences. In this matter, as in others, clergy can feel pressure from colleagues to accomplish some end considered desirable—the introduction of eucharistic vestments, perhaps, or the elimination of hymns deemed militaristic—regardless of the traditions and feelings of the community. John knew better, however, frequently quoting from the Revised Standard Version, "Of those whom thou gavest me I lost not one" (John 18:9). And I learned more than I knew by watching him.

A FIGHT WORTH HAVING

In the same way that in a declining church some have made a virtue of decline, as pointed out in chapter 3, so also in a conflict-racked church some make a virtue of conflict. Those who make virtues of decline and conflict are usually leading declining and conflicted parishes. On a church listserv recently there was a discussion of the merits of chairs versus pews. The conventional wisdom among many clergy nowadays is that chairs are preferable. It is also incontestable that many laypeople like the pews they have. One of the posts to the listserv strongly advocated the benefits of

chairs and ended by saying, "This is a fight worth having in a declining church."

The assertion, made in all seriousness, certainly brings the issue into focus. What *are* the fights that are worth having in a declining church? Since decline and conflict are closely correlated, is it in any way reasonable to suppose that adding to the conflict will turn the decline around? Or is the idea that fomenting conflict and presiding over decline are marks that you are fighting the good fight? Who are your opponents, then, but the remaining members of the diminishing flock? Despite the frequency with which one encounters this attitude, I simply cannot conceive of any sense in which this is a helpful way to think.

I say this with a great deal of sympathy for those in declining and conflicted parishes; they are in difficult situations indeed, and no one in such a place feels good about it. However, in the interests of clear thinking, and in the interests of the church itself, it must be pointed out that neither decline nor conflict is desirable. There may be situations where something other than ineffective leadership has caused conflict and decline, but decline and conflict are the typical indicators of bad leadership.

Think about this when you would like to embark on making something about your parish match more closely your mental picture of your ideal parish. In my current cure the offertory ritual is rather a mishmash of different traditions and customs. It would be entirely in my purview to "regularize" it, but instead of bringing it into line with my expectations and preferences, I have simply learned to do it as they do it and have accommodated myself to its rhythms. With all there is to do in that turnaround situation, this is, in my opinion, definitely *not* a fight worth having.

In a turnaround situation I suggest that there are virtually no fights worth having. If what you are doing is causing a fight to begin, examine your motives and your method carefully. Is what you are doing really essential to turning the situation around? Do not delude yourself on this point. Making things more like what you prefer is not necessarily the same thing as doing what is essential for the parish's good. If it is really essential, are you doing it in the most effective way? Here again, please do not let yourself off the hook too easily. Doing it the way that is easiest or most congenial to you is not necessarily the same thing as doing it in the way that will help turn the parish toward health while avoiding unnecessary conflict.

Clergy often absolve themselves of self-serving decisions by giving a theological gloss to their preferences. In the same listserv discussion about the merits of chairs versus pews, one contributor said, "Pews can't be moved and the space around them cannot be transformed. Chairs can do that. So should we strive to change and transform ourselves in Christ." I too believe that conversion and transformation in Christ are the goals (though I am not sure it comes about as a result of our striving), but I cannot agree that they will be attained more readily if the worship space has chairs rather than pews. Such thinking is closer to belief in magic than to sacramental theology.

Not every sign is an effective sign. Not every symbol actually communicates that which it symbolizes. Chairs may allow space to be configured for different uses, but that does not mean that people who sit in chairs on Sunday are more open to conversion and spiritual transformation. I know this truth all too well: I served a troubled parish with chairs. And no glib justification for what we would prefer, no matter how high-sounding, can substitute for clear thinking. The more we allow mental games like this to cloud our minds, the less effective we will be, and the more likely it is that what we do and how we do it will lead to conflict and decline.

So it is wise to choose your battles very carefully indeed, bearing in mind Dr. Martin Luther King, Jr.'s observation that "wars are poor chisels for carving out peaceful tomorrow." Wars seldom end as those who began them predicted, and wars of choice are the result of bad leadership. Your ministry will be much more effective if use your capital for something productive.

CENTRAL AUTHORITY
AND PERSONAL FAITH

Earlier I have referred to Charles Taylor's authoritative study of the changes over the last five hundred years "which takes us from a society in which it was virtually impossible not to believe in God, to one in which faith, even for the staunchest believer, is one human possibility among others."[33] One of Taylor's insights is of particular relevance to the discussion of how we act as leaders in the church because he sees a fundamental contradiction in the two things clergy have been trained to do. We want the members of our parishes to be wholehearted believers, and we also want them to accept the particular tenets and usages of the form of Christianity we profess.

> But the whole drive of the Reform movement, from the high Middle Ages, right through Reformation and counter-Reformation, right up through evangelical renewal and the post-Restoration Church, was to make Christians with a strong personal and devotional commitment to God and the faith. But strong personal faith and all-powerful community consensus can't ultimately consist together.[34]

This may be hard to accept, since for hundreds of years we clergy have conceived of our work as bringing people to wholehearted personal commitment to the faith within the consensus of the particular community to which we adhere. However, Taylor rightly insists on his point. Speaking of the Roman Catholic Church of the nineteenth century, he notes that it "has had trouble however, seeing how contradictory the goal ultimately is, of a Church tightly held together by a strong hierarchical authority, which will nevertheless be filled with practitioners of heartfelt devotion."[35] The mainline non-Roman Catholic churches of the West have a weaker central authority structure, but they generally have a very strong hierarchical authority in the kind of worship they permit. And both the liturgical and non-liturgical churches give the local pastor a great deal of power. The cleric is generally in charge of the congregation's program, and many clergy use their power to make the worship and educational life something that mirrors their preferences, regardless of the customs of the community.

The dynamic of reform is always this: into an existing community with its round of established rituals enters a reformer who feels she or he has a mandate to disrupt the customs and bring people to a wholehearted commitment to a new way of doing things. Add to this the magical thinking that allows us to imagine, for example, that replacing the pews in the church with chairs will somehow automatically make people more ready to be transformed in Christ, and the stage is set for misunderstandings, conflict, and decline.

Taylor's thesis is that either we can have a community devoted to the common rituals and the strong community consensus, whether the level of the consensus is at the congregational or denominational level, or we can have a community of personally committed believers of heartfelt devotion. Especially now, when "for many people today, to set aside their own path in order to conform to some external authority just doesn't seem comprehensible as a form of spiritual life,"[36] heartfelt devotion to all the tenets of the community's version of the faith will be a distinctly minority position.

The established churches of Christendom have vacillated at times between these two poles of personal commitment and community consensus. Because we cite approvingly Elizabeth Tudor's reluctance to make windows into people's souls, Anglicans have historically emphasized observance within the community consensus and have downplayed the necessity of strong personal commitment.

However, both the changes in the liturgy and the mostly misguided and ineffective efforts to stem the decline have made most clergy into real reformers. Many of us now understand our job as changing things, introducing things, suppressing things—in short, reforming things—until they reflect the unattainable ideal of a community of individuals who wholeheartedly embrace the community consensus we would like to impose.

I think this is a real difference in the self-understanding of most Episcopal priests today from that of priests up until the 1960s. In those days only the "spikes" felt they were on a mission to reform the church, introducing whatever Anglo-Catholic practices they felt they could get away with. Most clergy were more than satisfied with the Cranmerian language of the 1928 Prayer Book, surplice and stole on Communion Sunday, and tippet and hood the rest of the time.

Here is an example of the former self-understanding. In the mid-1980s a middle-aged man attended the 8 am Rite I celebration at our parish. He told John afterward that he was very confused by the service. He had not been in church for years, but he had always remembered that, thirty years before, one of John's predecessors had told his confirmation class that, whatever else might change in the church or in the world, the Order for Holy Communion would always, always begin on page 67 of the *Book of Common Prayer.* One simply cannot imagine similar words passing the lips of any priest today.

In the 1970s it became necessary to change the worship patterns of every Episcopal parish—a major reform effort. The mandate was indeed to disrupt the liturgical customs of probably 90 percent of parishes by replacing Morning Prayer as the principal Sunday service, and the remaining ten percent by altering the structure and language of the eucharistic liturgy. And the idea was that people were supposed not just to accept the changes, but to become wholeheartedly devoted to them.

With this mandate, and in the face of significant resistance from many congregations, it was easy for clergy to come to believe that the problem was "the way we've always done things." Instead of rejoicing that the congregation's liturgical customs were so meaningful to the people, many clergy tended to be impatient, and even disrespectful, of the people's established devotional patterns. In fact, clerical impatience with "the way we've always done things" in every aspect of parish life has become a principal way our conventional wisdom blames the people for the decline.

While the liturgical changes were being implemented, the general decline, which had begun a decade or more before, became impossible to ignore. In general the reform became conflated with the decline. Opponents of the liturgical changes said the new Prayer Book itself was causing the shrinkage. Adherents of the new liturgy became convinced that the "proper" enactment of the new liturgies would reverse the decline. A generation later, despite all the evidence to the contrary, many still believe that changing something external will turn things around.

The principal thesis of this book is that changing the words of the script and the blocking and staging will not turn things around. What is really communicated to the people in every service of worship is the spirit the liturgy conveys. A leader who sees herself as primarily a preserver of traditions she holds dear will convey disdain for any new ideas that the community puts forward. A leader who sees himself as a reformer will convey annoyance with the established ways and disparagement of things the community holds dear. I do not think either of these attitudes help turn around the decline. The spirit that I recommend emphasizes how God touches the individual in the community's worship and treads softly with respect to mandating anything. A celebration that observes the rubrics and respects the community's customs can then become a vehicle for the community's worship, not the point of the gathering.

CONTROL AS LITTLE
AS POSSIBLE

There are many common experiences in the formation of clergy and aspects of the parish situation that impel us toward becoming reformist control freaks. In seminary and in discussions with experienced clergy we can easily be drawn into the "us versus them" mentality. As parish clergy we learn to disdain the customs and usages that our professors disapproved of, despite the affection with which these customs are held by the people in the congregation. We have learned that it should be in our power to change all that, and to introduce those preferred symbolic actions that will make our Eucharists the perfect reflection of the heavenly banquet. We have been initiated into the mysteries of "higher" criticism and can therefore dazzle people with our scholarship. The parish programs—Sunday school, Bible study groups, midweek services, Lenten programs, and so on—are entirely in our control, and in most parishes will have had little consistency over the decades, so when we arrive as rector we can do what we like.

And as priests we find ourselves to be the main actors on the stage in leading the liturgy and preaching. The people hold us responsible for every particular in the performance of the services, complaining about the training of the acolytes and even, in one memorable instance, for the way choir members "gaped" at the congregation. If there is an adult server whose behavior does not conform to the norm, the people come to us with their complaint. And finally, for all the ink spilled in recent generations on the ministry of the laity, we know that while clergy control the parish program, lay ministry will remain, as the joke runs, precisely what the clergy say it is.

My suggestion is first, to acknowledge the reality of all these aspects of ordained parish ministry, and second, to resist their implications. The job of the clergy is not to control; our job is to foster. Our job is to create the conditions in which people will be moved to offer their gifts. Concentrate on the spirit, not the form, of the liturgy. It is not necessary, and, indeed, it is probably counter-productive to imagine that everything needs to be rebuilt. Live with the ambiguity of the less-than-perfect.

When I congratulated a friend on some aspect of the terrific job she is doing in her parish, she said, "Well, you know me. I don't control anything; I just let it happen around me." Then she added, "And of course I'm consumed with anxiety about it." I think that is about right. We are deeply aware of everything that is going on, bad and good, and we think we see ways of everything going well if people would just do what we want. But they won't, and besides, it is just as unhealthy for the clergy to control every aspect of parish life as it is for a lay pope to do so. We often have to let situations develop in their own way and just take what opportunities there are to make suggestions.

In a turnaround situation—and in many less dire situations—the real problems will be with how people relate to one another, not with what is done or the way it is done. Fights over the "what" and the "how" will be proxies for the underlying power struggles. Steering clear of mediating these battles is usually a good idea. Your goal is to work on other aspects of the situation; as the general situation improves, the urgency behind these squabbles will often diminish. Then things can be figured out on the basis of what works best rather than who wants what.

Most people do not like living with organizational ambiguity, but in conflicted situations trying to resolve the ambiguity often just worsens the conflict. At both Intercession and St. Mary's what happened to the offering after it was brought forward was the focus of heated conflict. At Intercession the issue was who had the combination to the safe into which the bags were placed after the presentation. At St. Mary's it was about whether the plates stayed in the sanctuary until the end of the service and who retrieved the money. Of course in neither case was the conflict really over the offertory ritual, but over who was in control. That issue could be decided only in other ways and in other venues as the situation improved and people began to be less anxious. Even in relatively healthy situations some will want you to adjudicate minor concerns, such as whether the choir should use the choicest parking spaces because they arrive early. I think it is often best not to engage. We are not Jesus, but we can imitate his refusal to be set as a judge or arbitrator over some things (Luke 12:14).

LIVE WITH WHAT
CANNOT BE FIXED

At a recent clergy gathering a newly ordained priest-in-charge related that after the All Souls' Day service a woman who had never attended that church before told him she was disappointed she could not receive communion because she had not been baptized. The priest, who is trying to reconnect the parish to the changing demographics of the area, said he had felt that conversation keenly.

The resulting conversation was instructive. First, understandably and correctly, his colleagues offered reassurance that the situation was not his fault, and that often what people say is the problem is not really the problem. The talk then went in two directions I did not expect: one priest said the woman should have asked to be baptized; others began to counsel their colleague not to adopt "open communion," a phrase that used to mean that members of one denomination could receive communion in another church, but that now more commonly refers to the practice of giving communion to those who have not been baptized.

At first I did not see the connection, but then I realized that both kinds of approaches were attempts to arrive at a "fix," to get out from the weight of being responsible for uncomfortable situations. If we take the position that the woman should have asked to be baptized if she wanted to receive communion, then we are not responsible for denying her communion; rather, she is responsible for her own exclusion. If we open communion to the unbaptized, then we have also fixed the situation. Commendably, in my opinion, neither the priest, a young man in his twenties, nor most of those present, were looking for a fix. He said after a while that he did not see an easy solution, but that he was "haunted" by his conversation with the woman. I think that is an appropriate response.

I doubt there would be a move toward open communion if Morning Prayer were still offered regularly. We have not thought through all the implications of scheduling the Eucharist as our only public worship in an age when it is more and more likely that seekers will not have been baptized.

Appropriate fixes are often not available to situations that put us clergy in uncomfortable positions. Trying to find a way out is like telling a grieving widow that it was God's will that her husband died. That deals with our own mental discomfort, but it comes at quite a collateral cost. There are plenty of situations, particularly in turnaround parishes, that must be lived with rather than resolved.

I HAVE NO AGENDA:
I JUST WANT IT TO WORK

Your effectiveness as a leader and your ability to negotiate dysfunctional interpersonal dynamics depend on how well your words and conduct genuinely convey that you have no agenda other than the turnaround and the thriving of the parish. The people need to see in you that kind of single-minded devotion to the future health of the parish they love. Many of them will not recognize it at first, even if you evince it. They will be too traumatized and too anxious. You will meet suspicion and mistrust. The people will probably not be able to believe right away that you are going to be different from the leaders who drove the parish into the ditch.

"I have no agenda; I just want it to work" is probably a fair summary of the method I believe is effective in bringing a parish back from the brink of failure. We can use it as a touchstone to test any project or idea we have. Is there anything self-serving in what we are thinking of saying or doing? Do I have any other agendas in mind here, apart from building the long-term good of the parish?

Failing situations do not give clergy much cover: everything is exposed. That's why dealing with a failing situation will be the most difficult work you have ever done. If people are very anxious, there will be no reservoir of goodwill when you arrive; rather, your every word and action will be scrutinized with the highest level of suspicion and bad faith. All your missteps will be caught. Even after many people begin to see that you are not after anything for yourself, the unhealthy actors in leadership roles will intensify their resistance to health. Even if your every word and action are patently selfless and aimed only at the long-term good of the parish—and they won't all be, because you are human—stories will grow behind your back of how duplicitous, conniving, and self-interested you are. These will hurt when you hear of them, and you have to be very careful in countering them. Usually it will be best to ignore the stories or to find a very low-key way of introducing the truth into the situation.

In each of the three failing situations I have dealt with, it has taken about two years before I began to feel that a significant corner had been turned. During that period every vestry meeting and many Sunday mornings made me feel that I was having no impact at all, and I spent a great deal of time feeling terrible.

This extended period in the wilderness is lonely. If my experience is any guide, the challenges of the interpersonal relationships will not only affect your feelings toward the parish, but they will also cause you to doubt your abilities and to wonder what the point of it all might be. The kinds of things people will say and do to you and to one another will likely cause your affection for the parish, so essential to being effective, to evaporate. Love is a decision, however, as much as a feeling. You may have to decide

to act as if you love the place during those periods when there is no love to be felt. If you do a very good job of that, two things may result. First, the feelings will return as things get healthier, and second, no one in the parish will suspect that you were "out of love" with the place for a time.

If turning a parish around were a different kind of work, these closing pages would be a rousing pep talk. As it is, they are more like the counsel one might give a loved one going through a very difficult situation: "I know how it feels." "These are some things that have helped me." "If you can resist doing the unhelpful things, you'll be glad later on."

I am not able to say all that might be useful in this work, and I have been far from a perfect practitioner of the approaches I have discussed. Nevertheless I do believe this: it *is* possible for parishes at the edge of failure to be revived. It may not be possible for every place that is failing to be brought back; we have discussed some of the factors that may preclude success in some places. If you are in a situation that needs to be turned around, I believe the method outlined here will help you in your work. May God bless us all in our efforts.

> May the graciousness of the LORD our God be upon us;
> prosper the work of our hands; prosper our handiwork.
> — PSALM 90:17

Endnotes

1. Gerald W. Keucher, *Humble and Strong: Mutually Accountable Leadership in the Church* (New York: Church Publishing, 2010).
2. Gerald W. Keucher, *Remember the Future: Financial Leadership and Asset Management for Congregations* (New York: Church Publishing, 2006).
3. Charles Taylor, *The Ethics of Authenticity* (Cambridge, Mass.: Harvard University Press, 1991), esp. 81–91.
4. Edith Wharton, quoted by James Elliott Lindsley, *This Planted Vine: A Narrative History of the Episcopal Diocese of New York* (New York: Harper & Row, 1984), 206.
5. Charles Taylor, *A Secular Age* (Cambridge, Mass.: The Belknap Press, 2007), 490.
6. Diarmaid MacCulloch, *Christianity: The First Three Thousand Years* (New York: Viking, 2010), 212.
7. MacCulloch, *Christianity,* 299.
8. Taylor, *A Secular Age,* 737–739.
9. Lindsley, *This Planted Vine,* 116.
10. J. P. K. Henshaw, *Memoir of the Life of the Right Reverend Richard Channing Moore DD* (Philadelphia: General Books, 1842), 26.
11. "The great Creator of the worlds," words from the *Epistle to Diognetus,* in *The Hymnal 1982* (New York: Church Hymnal, 1984), hymn 489.
12. C. Kirk Hadaway, *Episcopal Congregations Overview: Findings from the 2010 Faith Communities Today Survey* (March 2011), 2. Found at http://episcopalchurch.org/sites/default/files/downloads/episcopal_overview_fact_2010.pdf.
13. Lindsley, *This Planted Vine,* 303, in reference to Bishop Horace W. B. Donegan of New York.
14. Kenneth Johnson, "Demographic Trends in Rural and Small Town America" *Reports on Rural America* 1, no. 1 (Durham, N.H.: Carsey Institute, 2006), 1. See http://www.carseyinstitute.unh.edu/publications/Report_Demographics.pdf.
15. Hadaway, *FACT 2010 Overview,* 1.

16. Alex Ross, "Flummoxed: Struggles at City Opera and Across the Country," *The New Yorker* (May 9, 2011): 79.

17. Lindsley, *This Planted Vine*, 323.

18. Lindsley, *This Planted Vine*, 205.

19. See Keucher, *Humble and Strong*, for a fuller discussion.

20. Quoted in Sam Dillon, "4,100 Students Prove 'Small Is Better' Rule Wrong," *The New York Times* (September 27, 2010).

21. Words by James Montgomery, in *The Hymnal 1940* (New York: Church Pension Fund, 1940), hymn 419.

22. Adam Gopnik, "Sweet Revolution," *The New Yorker* (January 3, 2011): 57.

23. Ed Stetzer and Mike Dodson, *Comeback Churches: How 300 Churches Turned Around and Yours Can Too* (Nashville: B & H Publishing Group, 2007), 18.

24. George Barna, *Turn-Around Churches: How to Overcome Barriers to Growth and Bring New Life to an Established Church* (Ventura, Calif.: Regal Books, 1993), 85.

25. Andrew S. Dolkart, *Morningside Heights: A History of Its Architecture and Development* (New York: Columbia University Press, 1998), 68.

26. See Keucher, *Remember the Future*, 137–160, for a fuller discussion.

27. Keucher, *Remember the Future*, 115–131.

28. Taylor, *A Secular Age*, 490.

29. Hadaway, *FACT 2010 Overview*, 3; emphasis in the original.

30. Edwin H. Friedman, *Generation to Generation: Family Process in Church and Synagogue* (New York: The Guilford Press, 1985); Edwin H. Friedman, *A Failure of Nerve: Leadership in the Age of the Quick Fix* (New York: Seabury Books, 1999); Arthur Paul Boers, *Never Call Them Jerks: Healthy Responses to Difficult Behavior* (Bethesda, Md.: Alban Institute, 1999).

31. G. Lloyd Rediger, *Clergy Killers: Guidance for Pastors and Congregations under Attack* (Louisville: Westminster John Knox Press, 1997); Kenneth C. Haugk, *Antagonists in the Church: How to Identify and Deal with Destructive Conflict* (Minneapolis: Augsburg, 1988).

32. Dennis R. Maynard, *When Sheep Attack!* (Charleston: BookSurge Publishers, 2010).

33. Taylor, *A Secular Age*, 3.

34. Taylor, *A Secular Age*, 465–466.

35. Taylor, *A Secular Age*, 466.

36. Taylor, *A Secular Age*, 489.

CPSIA information can be obtained
at www.ICGtesting.com
Printed in the USA
LVHW032013221218
601428LV00001B/33/P